ACCELERATE
YOUR FAITH:
MIND, BODY AND SOUL

EVAJENKINS

Find Eva Jenkins on PowerHouse Couple on YouTube
for more tips on how to accelerate your faith.

Accelerate Your Faith is on Instagram and Facebook.

For more information, go to: powerhousecouple.org

MICHELLE/KAMRATH PUBLISHING
Copyright © 2020
Henderson, Nevada

ACCELERATE YOUR FAITH: MIND, BODY AND SOUL
by EVA JENKINS
ISBN-13: 978-1-7330368-2-5

I dedicate this book to my beautiful nieces:
Catalina, Madeline, and Gabriella,
and our future generations.

Special thanks to my Spanish editor:
Alma Rellano.

Special thanks for my book cover design:
Michelle Kamrath.

CONTENTS

The confirmation of this book:

In the process of getting our ministry together, I had it on my heart to write a book, but without direction or the name of the book. Then in a dream in November 2015, God gave me the title to this book. I remember asking Him, "Okay, God, now I need a picture of the cover," and then He gave me the vision for it. I woke up that morning, told my husband, and thanked God for giving me direction. Shortly after that, I was speaking at Toastmasters and decided to share a speech about faith. I knew that it would become my introduction for this book. Writing a book and the process of publication is new to me, but with God, He made all things possible. He led me to the right people, guided me in the writing process and where to invest my time. He also opened doors for me to share about faith, and made it easy to promote. He is not a respecter of persons, and I pray for those who want to write a book, that He will lead and guide you just as He did for me. The purpose of this book is for you not only to know what faith is but to start living out your confidence to new and higher levels. To move from faith to faith, and glory to glory. God has given us keys to the kingdom; now is the time to use them.

"Blessed are those who find wisdom, those who gain
understanding, for she is more profitable
*than silver and yields better returns than **gold**."*
Proverbs 3:13-14

It is my prayer for you to open your heart and let the Holy Spirit teach you the things you do not know. May you find wisdom and gain understanding through this book so that you may do the will of God in your life.

It is my passion to see the family unit restored. I know how important it is for spouses to be in unity in their marriages. When spouses agree, the enemy cannot create a foothold in the union. However, when there is contention, it can create a ripple effect to the children and in turn, create divisions and disunity. Thus, it does not resemble the Holy union God put together. I address how to keep unity in relationships in my upcoming book: Accelerate Your Faith in Marriage, along with my husband, who shares his point of view and faith for the husband's role.

Thank you to my husband who supported me in this journey of writing this book. Without you, I wouldn't have been able to achieve my dreams in finishing this book. Thank you for your love and encouragement and for supporting me to be the best me.

Thank you to Nick Loll for giving me suggestions and insight for the book.

Thank you to my parents: Douglas and Maria, for their discipline, love, and encouragement. I'm grateful for the road I've traveled and the experiences I've endured to be who I am today. And for my stepparents, Karen and David, for their love and time in my life. Thank you to my brother, Leon, and sister-in-law, Sophanara. You both have helped me throughout my life, and I will forever be grateful.

Thank you to my best friends, Jonathan Burke and Cynara Reynolds, for believing in me when nobody else did and being true friends in all seasons of my life.

I love you all very much.

Heavenly Father, I pray for those who read this book, to be filled with the Holy Spirit, gaining wisdom and insight on how to use their faith and share it with others. May they be used to the volume of the book that is written of them in heaven, in Jesus' name, Amen.

Eva Jenkins

CHAPTER ONE
MIND

IT BEGINS IN YOUR **MIND**

Let's imagine that your vehicle is your faith, and you are in the driver's seat, just like you are in the driver's seat of your car. Your hands are on the steering wheel, and you look down on the gearshift and think about moving it from park to drive. However, just like your vehicle, your faith does not move until you decide to use it. Faith begins in the mind, but for many of us, we have become hopeless, not thinking that our faith can do anything for us. We have let our disappointments settle into becoming our reality. The excitement and joy in life may become distant when everything "bad" seems to be happening around us. As we become adults, we may no longer know how to use our faith. Sometimes it is out of fear of saying the wrong thing or saying something in encouragement, but then that gets taken out of context, so we are afraid of what others may think or respond, in return. The unknown can become overwhelming for anybody, steering us in doubt and fear, paralyzing the possibility of what could be an enjoyable experience, if we knew where we were going.

I'm assuming we all have a car or have been in a vehicle before, so we know the experience can be pleasurable. However, many people choose not to get on the highway because they are afraid of other people and their driving. They tend to focus on what others are doing, rather than what they can do. Many times, we don't know what to expect from other people, so we may not share our faith. We tend to react in fear rather than give others hope because we may be too afraid to be wrong or judged since we live in a society that is self-approving.

Therefore, faith is based on the decisions we make. Let's begin with what is faith. Faith believes in the things we cannot see. It can be seen as hope for the future or beliefs that the best outcome will happen. Some people like to call it optimism. For Christians, our faith believes God is telling the truth, no matter how we may feel or what our circumstances are. We can hold on to His promises, and even though things may be a mess in our lives, we have the hope that we can trust in God, believing that He is bigger than our problems. Some people believe that if you think it, you can make it happen, but the focus is on self, like karma, what goes around comes around. Some believe what you do, determines the outcome. To illustrate, maybe you have read a fortune cookie, carried around a lucky rabbit's foot, or even collected two-dollar bills? We have the curiosity to see what something else may say about our determined future. It's as though our luck is in the premise of something else. Not thinking what we do or say may be in our own hands, but deep down, we believe something else may be guiding us, leading us and ultimately "in control." So mistakenly, we place our luck in the things we hope might grant us what we are asking. Usually, it is something tangible.

Now that you know what faith is you're probably asking, how do I use my faith? I mentioned earlier faith is based on the decisions we make; it starts in our minds. Even scripture states, "faith without works, is dead," so, faith is dead unless it is used. The decision starts with making a choice. Sometimes it requires us to try something different. However, no matter the circumstances, it is our right to choose. For example, we decided to get up this morning, and read this book. We chose to be attentive. We continuously make choices every day. We all make daily decisions, which means we are given the right to make our own choices. It is our self-will that allows us to choose. What we decide, we allow and approve of in our lives. We are, in a sense, creators in our decision making and whether we want to believe it, we can determine our outcome by the choices we make. If you choose not to use your vehicle or your faith, then you will never get to know how it works. You must decide to put the car in drive, put your foot on the accelerator, and go for it.

However, many times, doubt and fear stop us from using our faith. We can become disappointed in life's circumstances and become frustrated because things do not turn out as planned. If we're honest, we can quickly get discouraged. Just like in a car, we could be driving along, and everything seems fine, but then a check engine light comes on or all of a sudden, we get a nail in our tire and have to pull over to the side of the road. At that moment we have a decision to make. We could continue to drive our vehicles with the nail in the tires and cause further damage or we could pull over and assess the damage. Many times, we would rather keep going in life because we do not want to take the time to stop. We think it will slow our process and in our minds, we can tell ourselves, "Busy is good." If we are too busy to slow down, then we must ask ourselves, who are we doing our work for? God wants us to acknowledge our hurt and tend to what is damaged or bent inside of us. He wants us to face our fears and doubts. To move past the discouragement, we must allow ourselves to take risks. We need to take the chance to do something different that isn't our norm and give ourselves the courage to keep going. God calls us to do the impossible. He says without faith it is impossible to please Him. That means faith is the only way to please Him. However, many of us fall into doubt and fear and focus on the wrong possibility.

What would happen if we shifted our focus and not just thought about using our faith but knew that there were no limits or boundaries to what our faith could do? Instead of focusing on what we aren't good at, we focus on what we have hope in. Instead of focusing on how someone may be sick, we focus on the possibility of a healing miracle. Instead of focusing on the amount in our bank account, we speak God's Word that we have more than enough in Christ Jesus. Instead of focusing on the "should haves" or "what if's," we focus on the endless possibilities of just being.

The discouragement makes us focus on how we don't see the benefit in being hopeful. We become hopeless in a sense and turn to ourselves for the answer or comfort rather than believing there is a truth or meaning to our disappointment. We tend to rationalize the outcome, discounting there was any hope in the first place by summing it up as a possible "coincidence." We tend to count our wrongs and mistakes more than celebrating our victories. In a sense, we have slowly been depreciating our sense of self, values, beliefs, and ultimately, our faith. However, don't lose hope, with the tools in this book and workbook. I hope our faith will be ignited into practice and may we know that we hold the key to making it happen.

With vision, our lost dreams can be restored by our faith. We are in the driver's seat of what we want to see through and where we decide to go. It begins as a choice and deciding to do it. Activating our faith is taking a risk at something we may not have done before. It starts with a decision in our minds for the best positive outcome, despite our circumstances or problems. It is living out our beliefs, in which, by faith, we were made to do the impossible.

Believing Creates Possibility

Haven't tangible things failed us long enough? I had put my trust into so many false hopes, that when I decided to put my trust in God, I finally started seeing things change. The enemy always wants us to believe that there is "nothing new under the sun," but with Jesus, He makes all things new. He gives new hope, new life, new aspirations, and new relationships. Jesus is the One who makes all things possible.

How quickly do we forget that God has put His Spirit in us, to partner with Him, and to know what He is doing. When Jesus performed miracles, He mentioned He did what He saw the Father do, and nothing was apart from Him. What would happen if we listened to God like this? What would happen if whatever we did, we did it because it was His will for our lives? He has said, He knows the plans He has for us, plans to prosper us and not to harm us. That means, when we listen to God, it is for our good. He wants to bless and prosper us. Prosperity in health, wealth, and relationships can be added to our lives as He is with us in all these things. Immanuel means, "God with us."

We cannot move forward in our faith if we do not understand who God is. If we relate God to being angry, far and distant, then we will behave as though He does not see us or know us, and we can mistake

Him to be an impersonal God. However, if we see Him as close, loving, and caring, we are more likely to understand His goodness. We relate to others the way we believe He relates to us. Knowing His nature, makes us realize who we are and what we possess as His son or daughter. We have the authority to do all things through Him who strengthens us, and it is the power of the Holy Spirit to lead us to all truth and work on behalf of His authority.

We can move from believing to knowing who we are in Him. When we know who we are, we act different, we respond with boldness and confidence, and it comes from a reverent fear of Him. Fearing God rather than "man," allows us to shift from pleasing man to pleasing God. To know the difference, we may be given experiences in our relationships to know how to act and react in a way that allows us to choose in whom we will please, God or man. It is good to gain knowledge in boundaries and the way they work in our relationships. To move to a higher level, this knowledge has to be in place. Discernment is applicable during this process. Knowing that our decisions are either motivated by fear or love will help us understand how to place boundaries in our relationships. We can ask God for the discernment if we are doing something out of fear (fear of not being liked, fear of losing someone, fear of being hurt, fear of being known or unknown, fear of missing out, or fear of not being good enough) or love (no personal gain).

In all my decisions, I have found it best to ask God what pleases Him. Fear can paralyze our faith and stop us from doing something for God. Many times we can be afraid, just as the unprofitable servant was fearful, "I was afraid and went and hid your talent in the ground."[1] This kind of fear can tempt us to be lazy, not to try or become complacent and think we need to hoard things in order to prosper, which is wrongful thinking. Having a reverent fear of God is knowing that He has our good in His mind. To live above my feelings, I must remember what God has done for me in Christ Jesus. Knowing what He has done for me, creates such joy in my heart and confidence, knowing that since He gave me Jesus, what else won't He give me according to His riches and glory? God loves us so much that He even became the atonement for our sins when the Israelites could not keep the Law. He humbled Himself to be born on earth as a man, having the full nature of God so that we may be in relationship with Him. To understand the Law of Christ, we must first understand what Law the Israelites were doing to obtain righteousness.

The Israelites were given the Mosaic laws from God, which included making an atonement for sin, making sacrifices to the Lord, certain traditions like Passover, the days of Unleavened Bread, and the feast of the Tabernacle.

Know that a man is not justified by observing the law, but by faith in Jesus Christ. So we, too, have put our faith in Christ Jesus that we may be justified by faith in Christ and not by observing the law, because by observing the law no one will be justified.
Galatians 2:16

We see that the law cannot justify or make any man righteous, which is why God sent His Son to fulfill the requirements of the law for all those who believe in Him. Christ became the end of the law by living

---
1   Matthew 25:25

a sinless life and becoming the sacrifice (blood was shed) on the cross. Faith in Jesus has satisfied the demands of the law and now restores us into a loving relationship with God. However, this does not mean we have permission to sin. On the contrary, this means we conduct ourselves as righteous because we have the Holy Spirit living in us to do His will through us. Because Jesus Christ fulfilled the law, we too can be above reproach in how we communicate and handle things. We are now considered to be living under grace and not under the law.

Many people assume that since the Ten Commandments were given in the Old Testament, they do not apply to us in the New Testament. However, there is a connection between the Old and the New, in which when crafted together, brings understanding. His commandments keep us from falling into calamity. We do not do His commandments to obtain righteousness, for we are already righteous through Jesus Christ (for those who believe). Jesus didn't fulfill the commandments to give us a pass to sin. If someone claims, "I know God," but doesn't obey God's commandments, that person is a liar and is not living in the truth.[2] Jesus even spoke these words:

> *Those who accept my commandments and obey them are the ones who love me. And because they love me, my Father will love them. And I will love them and reveal myself to each of them.*
> John 14:21

> *For this is the love of God, that we keep His commandments and His commandments are not burdensome.*
> 1 John 5:3

---

2   1 John 2:4 [NLT]

Jesus gave us a new commandment to love others as He loved us. The passage above says, the love of God is to keep His commandments, which means when we obey His commandments, we love Him. We cannot assume we know how to love others if we do not know or understand His way to do that. When Jesus gave the commandment to love God with all our hearts, strength, and minds and to love others as ourselves, how do we know the right way to love God if we do not learn what He likes and dislikes? We can love others like we love ourselves, but what if we continue in our approach to love others? Would you think they would know you love them? Probably not.

We fail to love others well because we assume people are like us. We expect people to be like us but when we are aware of differences we freeze or are confused about how to build intimate connections. We become bewildered on how to love others in a way they know they are being loved. When we understand love, according to God, then the world will know us (Believers) by our love.[3] Would it be good enough to do it our way or is there a way that with God, we can show His love?

Jesus promises that He will love us, reveal Himself to us, and then our Father will also love us. The commandments are not meant to withhold anything good from us, which sounds reasonable. However, for some reason, we may twist what was meant to be "good," to now be perceived as "bad." We may want to believe that grace gives us the mandate to do what we choose, however, it doesn't. Thinking this way, increases our mindset to think we know what is best, but we don't. It is written, "'For My thoughts are not your thoughts,

---

3   John 13:35

21

nor are your ways My ways,' says the Lord. 'For as the heavens are higher than the earth, so are My ways higher than your ways, and My thoughts than your thoughts.'"[4] To walk by faith, we walk according to the Spirit, not by law or letter. His commandments help us to learn how to serve Him well with the right kind of heart and not in our way, which brings death. There is a way that appears to be right, but in the end, it leads to death.[5] In the last days, lawlessness will be increased, and the love of many will grow cold.[6] We are to protect our minds and focus on what is true, lovely, noble, pure, admirable, excellent, or praiseworthy.[7] This even means protecting our faith by being obedient to His commandments. Let's take a look at His commandments from Exodus 20.

"You must not have any other god but me."[8] In this day and age, the term god, seems muddled. For those who may not know what "other god" means, I define it as, anything I do or talk about more than God. The thing that I do most can be considered a god: work, television, children, spouse, family, or ourselves. It is easy to have other gods before Him because we can become immersed in our daily priorities. We may even put our spouses as "gods," due to our thoughts and actions trying to make our spouses love us by doing or saying the right thing for them to be "happy." It can also be trying to be "perfect" for them or trying to get them to meet our emotional needs. It's the same way with children. We may ask our children to do things for us for selfish reasons. For example, we look to our children to comfort us when we are sad, or to make us laugh or

---

4   Isaiah 55:8-9
5   Proverbs 14:12
6   Matthew 24:12
7   Philippians 4:8
8   Exodus 20:3

smile. We tell them to stay close to us because of our fear or anxiety of being alone in the home but, we fail to ask God to comfort our needs. We have to be mindful as to what we are doing and the motive behind why we do it, and make sure the person, place or thing does not replace God to meet an emotional or physical need.

"You must not make for yourself an idol of any kind or an image of anything in the heavens or on the earth or in the sea."[9] God does not want to be carved into something man-made. God is not confined to this earth, and He does not want to be misrepresented. Other cultures have made images of their gods, but with our God, we must believe He is with us at all times, and therefore, we do not need to make an image of Him. Deuteronomy states:

> *"You must not bow down to them or worship them, for I, the Lord your God, am a jealous God who will not tolerate your affection for any other gods. I lay the sins of the parents upon their children; the entire family is affected—even children in the third and fourth generations of those who reject me. But I lavish unfailing love for a thousand generations on those who love me and obey my commands."*
> Exodus 20:5-6

God has mercy on those who will choose to listen to Him. Not only does He have mercy for those who obey Him but also for their children. So when we choose to listen to God we aren't just doing it for ourselves, we are doing it for future generations. Wouldn't it be great to leave something behind for generations to come, whom

---

9   Exodus 20:4

you may never meet until eternity? They will know that you are the one who set them up on the path of righteousness and because of you, they do not have to stumble, because they will know the Lord, their God, Jesus Christ. That sounds like a victorious legacy to me. Putting in the hard work sets up the next generations for success, which gives them something to walk into! Isn't it easier to continue the fight when you already know the victory has been accomplished? It's because we know others have gone before us, that we subconsciously have the motivation to keep going, because one person's act of obedience is authentically a part of us.

"You must not misuse the name of the Lord your God."[10] Even as a child, I remember hearing, "Do not say the Lord's name in vain." Saying the Lord's name in vain is not a way to show you love Him. When bad things happen, people are quick to say His name in vain, and it does nothing for us. So why say it at all? Why mention a name that is Holy and misuse it as a cuss word? Combining His name with a curse word does not set Him apart as Holy, but it makes us blend in with those who do not believe in Him. It discounts what we have inside us. We may act like it's just a word, but honestly, it's not. My God's name is HOLY and should be treated as such. Words matter to God, and either you are cursing yourself or allowing blessings to flow. We even misuse the word, *Holy*. Everything unholy usually comes out of a holy statement. When we truly learn to honor and respect God and love Him deeply, our words should be the first thing we work on, for it can either destroy or restore what God has for us.

"Remember to observe the Sabbath day by keeping it holy."[11] You

---

10   Exodus 20:7
11   Exodus 20:8

have six days each week for your ordinary work, but the seventh day is a Sabbath day of rest dedicated to the Lord your God. On that day, no one in your household may do any work. This includes you, your sons and daughters, your male and female servants, your livestock, and any foreigners living among you. For in six days, the Lord made the heavens, the earth, the sea, and everything in them; but on the seventh day, he rested. That is why the Lord blessed the Sabbath day and set it apart as holy.[12] It is time to remember that God can do what we cannot do in our week. It gives us reliance on Him, knowing that it is by His strength and powerful arm that He can accomplish more than we could ever think or imagine. Today, it is difficult to consider the Sabbath because we are told to work hard, work long hours, and always be available to work for us to be successful.

This thinking is not true, but because not keeping the Sabbath seems logical (especially when we think it's all about money), we mistakenly perceive it to be true. Not everything that looks or sounds good is actually good for us. That includes not keeping the Sabbath. We must remember the land belongs to the Lord, and He blesses those who are faithful to Him. Just look at Chick-fil-A fast-food chain. They are not open on Sundays, but God has blessed them as one of the most sustainable restaurants. Consider Jesus healing on the Sabbath. Some may consider healing to be work, but to Jesus, it was what He saw His Father doing, and considered it right to do. To take care of others is doing the Lord's work. Consider in your heart why you do what you do and see if it is for the Lord on the Sabbath. Another way to consider if it's work is to evaluate your actions in what you're doing. If you are more worried about making a "quota" or trying to make more money, it is considered not trusting God in what He can

---

12   Deuteronomy 5:12

do. Learn to trust in the Lord in this area and enjoy the rest.

"Honor your father and mother."[13] Then you will live a long, full life in the land the Lord your God is giving you."[14] I had not thought about this much until I was older. I did not think this mattered as a child because although I was told to show respect, (by not talking back or showing too much emotion), I did not see this respect modeled in my home, so I did not think much about honoring my mother or father. But no matter our perspective, this is something important to God and something we should do, even if we do not feel like it or think we ought to. It's out of obedience we decide to walk in faith. When you honor your parents, you are ultimately honoring God since you are obeying His commandment. Now, as an adult, I have a different perspective, and I look for ways I can honor my parents. I may fail at times, but I keep doing what I can do for them in their love language. It could even be as simple as doing your best, living your life to your best ability, and believing they did the best they could for you with what they had.

"You must not murder."[15] God does not want us to take someone else's life. We can even murder in our hearts, wishing someone would die, speaking evil about them, and so forth. I believe although we fall short, God's mercy covers us when we accept His Son and turn from our sin. There is so much heartbreak between all families when someone takes another person's life. Let God be the judge of someone's soul. We are called to not take revenge on someone else or to use the sword. Remember this truth, He speaks, "Vengeance is

---

13   Exodus 20:12
14   Deuteronomy 5:16
15   Exodus 20:13

mine; I will repay."[16]

"You must not commit adultery."[17] To not fall into sexual sin, takes a lot of self-awareness, prayer, and self-control. We are tempted because of our sin, not because of someone else. To protect ourselves from sinning against God, we must set up barriers or boundaries to what we allow ourselves to see and do. For example, if pornography is a temptation, then we could set channels on the television that dictate what we watch so nothing can influence our decisions or thoughts. If alcohol is a temptation, then we can set a boundary where we tell ourselves, "I will not drive past regular bar hang-outs," or "I will not hang-out with so and so." This will help us overcome distorted thinking. Boundaries provide guidelines that help reestablish thoughts according to God's will.

When our subconscious minds acknowledge a boundary, we will instinctively begin to question our decisions and how they align with God's desires for us. Boundaries help create a sense of awareness around our temptations where the process of reevaluation begins and thinking changes. When our thinking changes so will our response. Think about what you would want your best friend to do if they were trying to get help with their temptation and then do it for yourself. Treat yourself with love and care but not at someone else's expense. Look at the bigger picture of the lives you will be ruining instead of thinking about your selfish desires and what you would want for a brief moment. Accountability with a trusted friend and having a godly counselor can help with the process of dissecting the root causes of this struggle.

---

16   Romans 12:19
17   Exodus 20:14

"You must not steal."[18] Money has taught us different lessons in life. For example, some people have been taught, "The more you have, the more people will want to be around you or be like you." Others have been taught, "Money is the root of evil. The more you have, the more you want, and you will never be satisfied." Some people have stolen things because it was a means of survival, and for others, it was for power. But God does not want us to value things and especially money, more than Him. Ask yourself, do I need this? Can I be happy for someone else and their success? Can I trust God to meet all my needs? Are you willing to train yourself to be content in all things? Money is a great tool to help us learn how to overcome greed and selfishness. Since we do not take it with us when we die, we must learn how to steward it God's way.

"You must not testify falsely against your neighbor."[19] Your word is supposed to bring truth, and you are either sowing blessings or curses. When you testify falsely, you are lying not just to people, but to God. God is very serious when it comes to those who lie. God will not even accept liars to enter the kingdom of heaven.[20]

"You must not covet your neighbor's house." "You must not covet your neighbor's wife, male or female servant, ox or donkey, or anything else that belongs to your neighbor."[21] To *covet* means, *to desire, to have or yearn to have something.* Covetousness is like stealing, and it's a matter of the heart. God does not want us to take what does not belong to us. Instead of listening to the yearning or desire, ask God to take away the desire and help you align your

18	Exodus 20:15
19	Exodus 20:16
20	1 Corinthians 6:9-11
21	Exodus 20:17

desires to His.

"Love one another."[22] Love one another as Jesus has shown His love to His disciples. We are to mimic Him, imitate Him, and as believers, we are called to love like Him. The Son of God instructed us to "love your neighbor as yourself."[23] Jesus gave Judas a kiss, knowing he was going to betray him with money. Jesus did not point out his sin of greed and pride but let him do what was in his heart to do and let the will of His Father do what was meant to happen. Sometimes we try to control people because they have sin in their lives. We hold them at a higher standard and think they would be "perfect" if they go to church. We all have stigmas about people, but is it necessary? How do we know whether it is God's will or the enemy getting in our way? Ultimately, the Lord gives us over to our selfish desires.[24] If you find your heart hardening, humble yourself and ask God to soften your heart. I have done this throughout my walk with Him. Having a humble, meek, and pure heart before Him gives us the capacity to love as He does. Even as His friend, we do as He commands us. "If you keep My commandments, you will abide in My love, just as I have kept My Father's commandments and abide in His love."[25]

God can do just as much with a new believer as He can with a seasoned believer. We must not be judgemental with age or race, but do what Jesus came to do, which was to be about His Father's business. God has given us a relationship with Him through His Son. He has given us the power to set captives free and loose those who are in bondage. *Captivity* means *confinement, imprisonment,* or

---

22   John 13:34
23   Mark 12:31
24   Romans 1
25   John 15:10

custody. *Loose* means *detached from something*. *Bondage* means the *state of being a slave*, and it looks like oppression. Imprisonment is not just a physical place but is confinement in the mind of unhealthy thinking. When disasters strike, unexpected things happen, and feelings start to overwhelm people, what they need is Jesus. They can find Him in you. Jesus prayed:

> *"May they also be in us so that the world may believe that You have sent me. I have given them glory that You gave me, that they may be one as we are one: I in them and You in me. May they be brought to complete unity to let the world know that You sent me and have loved them even as You have loved me."*
>
> John 17:21-23

If we don't know who is in us, how can we give hope to a world that needs us? "There is no fear in love, but perfect love casts out fear because fear involves torment. But he who fears has not been made perfect in love."[26]

"And I know that His command is everlasting life."
– Jesus John 12:50

For the law came by Moses; grace and truth came through Jesus Christ.[27] Jesus gave us power to fulfill His commandments. Grace has given us an internal ability to accomplish His will. Now we can walk in freedom because of what Jesus has accomplished when He died on the cross. He gave us hope to endure through love.

---

26   1 John 4:18
27   John 1:17

Many Christians today talk about "possessing the land" God has for them. In Deuteronomy, we see God instructing Moses to teach the people statutes and judgments so that they will do them in the land they are going to enter. The Israelites were full of fear after the commandments were given, when it started to thunder, and they saw flashes of lightning. Moses encouraged the people not to be afraid telling them God has come in this way to test them, and so that their fear of Him would keep them from sinning.[28]

God tests us, for what is in our hearts and He sees whether we keep His commandments or not. This keeps us humble. Our fear of God should keep us from sinning. This is powerful. To renew our thinking, we must do something differently, even if it scares us. To change or shift gears in life, we must learn to rely on God rather than on ourselves or man. We learn from the world what we "need," but when that fails us, we may become confused, distraught, disappointed, or go into a self-protection mode. This keeps us from moving forward. If our fear of God hasn't stopped us from sinning, then we still have some work to do internally.

If we believe Jesus is the same yesterday, today and forever,[29] then we must understand that the commandments still stand for today. It does not give us a pass to sin, thinking that all we need to do is to ask for forgiveness and having God's grace means we can still do things our way. We are to put on the new self, which is being renewed in knowledge in the image of our Creator, in true righteousness and holiness.[30] The best way to know Him is to read His Word.

---

28   Deuteronomy 8:2 paraphrased
29   Hebrews 13:8
30   Colossians 3:10, Ephesians 4:24

All Scripture is given by inspiration of God, and is profitable for doctrine, for reproof, for correction, for instruction in righteousness, that the man of God may be complete, thoroughly equipped for every good work.

2 Timothy 3:16-17

To accomplish His will on earth, we need to find out what He likes and dislikes. Knowing that He will receive our love if we keep His commandments is a great way to start living a life of faith.[31] We need to remind ourselves that it's not a matter of what we do, instead, it's a matter of the heart. What is in our hearts will be shown in what we do. If we love Him, we will obey His commandments. We are even considered blessed when we do His commandments. "Blessed are those who do His commandments, that they may have the right to the tree of life, and may enter through the gates into the city."[32] We can think of the commandments as a gift from God. It brings us freedom when we obey His commandments, because not obeying Him brings us unsettled hearts because ultimately, we are sinning against Him. When we know what God has given us, then we know that God is more than capable to accomplish the work He started in us. But first, let's focus on why believing is so important.

Jesus gave his disciples a promise, "Because of your unbelief; for assuredly, I say to you, if you have faith as a mustard seed, you will say to this mountain, 'Move from here to there,' and it will move; and nothing will be impossible for you."[33] Since Jesus told this to His disciples, we know as long as we do not doubt, we can do all things. One of the first tactics the enemy used on Eve was to get

---

31   1 John 15:5
32   Revelation 22:14
33   Matthew 17:20

her to doubt what God had said about not eating the fruit from the tree of the knowledge of good and evil. God had told Adam not to eat from it, for in the day that he does eat of it he shall die. God gave the command to Adam, but the serpent went to Eve. She was not in God's presence when He told Adam. The serpent questioned what God had said, insinuating God was keeping them from something good by stating, "For God knows that in the day you eat of it your eyes will be opened and you will be like God, knowing both good and evil."[34] What they failed to realize was that they were already like God, made in His image. That is why it is essential to know God and how He made us, in His likeness.

God has made everything for a purpose on purpose. The man is to represent God as the image and glory of God, and women is to represent her husband as the glory of man.[35] God had given Eve the ability to give birth. The man carries the seed, but only through women can there be a reproduction. God put a purpose in women that only they carry. It's not just to reproduce, but it's also to birth something spiritually when they know who they are in Him. The enemy cannot stop women from reaching their full destiny. Man can reproduce who they are in their wives if their seed (fruitfulness in their lives) is good and lays on good soil. Their wives are their reflections.

There are constant (good and bad) seeds being planted in us, but God gives the increase to fully manifest His glory through us. We can release to Him, what is not of Him, so we can be light as He is light. We cannot be everything He sees we are, until we know what we

---

34   Genesis 3:5
35   1 Corinthians 11:7

carry on the inside of us. We must be willing to renew our minds, not just to know, but believe we are holy and righteous. We must know our position in His mighty Kingdom as being made a little lower than the angels. [36] When we get to heaven, we will actually judge the angels, meaning we will be higher than them in our resurrected bodies, since we are heirs with Christ and sons and daughters of the living God. [37] When Christ was resurrected, we were seated with Him, and no matter what our circumstances may look like, we have power and dominion over all areas of our lives. [38] If we suffer, we shall also reign with Him: if we deny Him, He also will deny us, if we believe not, yet He stays faithful: He cannot deny Himself. [39]

We Have Power

Believers are seated *with* Christ. The words we speak come with authority and power from the Holy Spirit, and we can take our authority or let the enemy take our authority (we will get to examples later). We must put our faith into action by taking a risk to see our God-given authority, which begins with knowing our position seated in Christ. Believers are seated next to Jesus, who is our Groom, and we are His bride. He is madly in love with us, sings over us, rejoices and dances over us. Imagine singing to your child and celebrating with your child when they do something good or for the first time. This is how excited God gets over us. However, just like a child, we may continually reject and rebel against Him.

We don't always understand His ways and are unsure if He is really

---

36   Hebrews 2:7-9
37   1 Corinthians 6:3, John 1:12
38   Ephesians 2:6
39   2 Timothy 2:12-13

good based on the pain that we see or the suffering we may endure. We try to figure out God by relating Him to our earthly parents, caretakers, friends or what is happening in the world. We may fail to understand who He is because of what we have seen and compare Him to what we have in our lives. He tells us that His ways are not our ways, and they are above our thinking, just as heaven is above the earth. Because we don't *know* Him, or He is a *mystery* to us, we minimize what He can do for us and tend to think He is less powerful than the enemy. We may *reason* God must be powerless.

However, the enemy is a *created* being and has no power over God. He only has power that God gives him. Nothing compares to our God, He has no opposite, and He has no rival. God is in control and has the utmost power. He did not choose to Father another part of creation (animals, sea, land, or angels). God *chose* us to be in relationship with Him as our *loving* Father. We must remember that He can use non-believers as much as He can use believers to accomplish His will. Yet subconsciously we may easily compare Him to our earthly father (or primary caretaker) or lack thereof. If our experiences were not good, it could lead to an unhealthy way of viewing our Father in heaven.

I have always wanted to understand why
my dad did not believe in God,
I had assumed that it was because his dad
died when my dad was only eighteen.
Was he mad at God?
Did he think that if God was *loving*,
then he must have forgotten him?

When I came into my faith,
I was so excited to tell my dad about what God
had done for me and what I was learning.
However, I was also that person who thought
that the world was going to end
on the Mayan calendar day in 2012
and wanted to make sure my dad knew Jesus
before the date so I knew I would be able
to see him again in heaven.

But my dad informed me that people try
to guess when the world might end
every ten years or so, and it never happens.
He was right, it didn't happen,
and it still tries to get predicted today.
I had realized, it wasn't what he
needed to hear to come to faith.

It is better to give your cares to God than worry about when the world might end. But what about those we love? What about the souls that have yet to be saved? I hate thinking that I do not know where my dad would go if he were to die unexpectedly today. It is a disheartening feeling to know that someone has rejected Jesus and will go to hell. Instead, I choose to believe that God can and will work in his heart, no matter how long it may take. A plethora of times, we can run out of patience with people, but our Father is longsuffering, slow to get angry, gentle, and kind to us. He knows what we need to come to Him and how long it will take before we make the decision to accept Jesus as our Lord and Savior. There are many debates as to whether or not your whole household will be saved once you become a believer because of what is written in Acts 16:31. It states, "So they said, "Believe on the Lord Jesus Christ, and you will be saved, you and your household." What I know about God is that He is much more merciful than we are since He wants no one to perish.[40]

To know God as your personal loving Father, you must forgive your earthly dad for any offenses that may have happened to you. You cannot see or know God as *loving* or perhaps even as a *Father* when your earthly dad has hurt you in *any way*. I can understand the term "fatherless nation" with many fathers not taking the responsibility of their children, not wanting to pay child support, or helping out, or using their children for their selfish benefit. There are many ways in which fathers and mothers have not been appropriate in their relationships with their children. Maybe, your father wasn't there for you as a child. Perhaps, he didn't say anything to build you up as you were becoming an adult, or he was very absent-minded or distant. No matter what has happened in your childhood, your Heavenly Father wants you to not just *know* but *believe* to whom you belong. Even if your earthly parents openly have said they did not want you, you have been chosen by God.

God has Chosen You!

Even though others may have hurt you, God loves you and cares deeply about you, for He even takes the time to count the hairs on your head! I know my earthly dad would never do that! When we don't forgive, we can turn to ourselves to make us feel better or pretend like we are not bothered by it. We can act like we have

---

40   2 Peter 3:9

forgiven because we try not to think about our hurt, but in reality, it's still there lingering, subconsciously.

In my hurt, I learned how easy it was to brush things off
to the side, pretend like I'm not hurt by what others say,
or act like everything was fine when it wasn't.
It's much easier to cut people out of our lives,
than face the pain or confrontation to make things better.
I would put up roadblocks and not allow people to get too close,
and when I felt threatened, I would gossip or criticize.
It was my way to protect myself from getting hurt again,
but deep down I was allowing that hurt to turn
into fear which led me to react in doubt that they care for me.

Eventually, I became paranoid in my thinking,
that they are out to 'get' me and
hopeless in my thinking that nobody likes me.
I was fending for me. I put on a smile wherever I went,
to look perfect on the outside,
but inside I was deeply hurting and longing for someone
to rescue me from my hurt and pain,
but that superhero never came.
I masked my feelings rather than telling people the truth.
I would make up lies that sounded better to me
than explaining the real reason why I was hurt or angry.
I didn't think anyone would understand.
I thought I was the only one thinking this way.
Everyone else looked so "put" together,
I thought something must be wrong with me.
Because I didn't feel approval at home,
I yearned for people to like me.
I thought about what they might like to hear

for them to be my friend.
Looking back at this, now I can see how in that process,
I lost a sense of who God made me to be,
due to trying to fit into other people's perceptions.
We can even make promises to ourselves
to not get hurt again and subconsciously
we become controlling of others.
We do this because we do not want to experience
that same hurt again, but we are actually the ones
doing the hurting because of our own hurt.

Taking control of our hurt and not giving it to God is holding an offense, bitterness, and resentment. It is not allowing God to become part of our healing process in our hurt, pain, and anger. We must remember, hurt people, hurt people. We must be willing to go through the pain of why we are hurt and understand the root cause of it, and then release it to God so we don't damage other relationships based on our past.

Forgiveness is vital for us to grow closer to God. The sooner we forgive, the sooner we can be healed from our pain. The sooner we acknowledge that we cannot do it in our strength, the quicker God can do His part to heal our hearts. The more we do things our way, the more He'll give us over to our ways and the more we'll fall

> deeper
>
> and
>
> deeper
>
> into the pit we dug for ourselves. The fastest way to

give our power over to Satan is to hold an offense and to think this life is about us. When we forgive, we are releasing that person to God and God will forgive us for our sins. If we forgive other people when they sin against us, our heavenly Father will also forgive us, but if we do not forgive others their sins, our Father will not forgive our sins.[41] When people hurt us knowingly or unknowingly, we must forgive them. Otherwise, we are allowing the enemy to enter into our minds and hearts and permitting him to give us doubt, confusion, and strife. We let him do this because the opposite of forgiveness is bitterness, and we can become bitter when we choose not to forgive.

Forgiveness is a Choice, not a Feeling

We cannot wait until we feel like forgiving before making our move, otherwise, we are still choosing not to forgive, and it's easier to be misled into the wrong thinking and behavior when we do this. Even Jesus forgave those who nailed Him to the cross and asked for His Father to forgive them because they did not know what they were doing.[42] Many times, when an offense happens, the person who has offended us is so caught up in their junk that they have no idea that they wronged us in any way. When we get offended, it's something we need to deal with and not something that someone else needs to change for us, so we feel better about ourselves. When we tell people how to act to make us feel more comfortable, that is manipulation and control. God wants us to work out what is in our hearts. If we become bothered by a statement or circumstance, we are to look within ourselves and ask, "Where is this coming from? Why am I offended?" And then profess to the Lord our hurt (from where the hurt originated) and say, "I choose to forgive this person for (and

---

41   Matthew 6:14-15
42   Luke 23:34

be specific)." Sometimes we do not put ourselves in other people's shoes enough to think or know how others might feel by our response or reaction to them. To love deeply is to show compassion. Jesus demonstrated that on the cross. He had so much compassion for them because they didn't know any better; they seriously thought they were doing the right thing. They thought they were doing themselves a good service, but they were dead wrong. We cannot let what others do dictate how we live in Christ.

To have a powerful life we must understand why we react or respond to certain words and circumstances. We control how we react to a person, even when we're offended. It's still a choice to choose love rather than to respond in fear and hurt. We control how to dictate our emotions and decide what to do with them. We are more than capable of living a life above our offenses, resentment, and bitterness, but we must surrender our pride in the process. If pride or satisfaction is a big mountain to conquer, know that God has called you to move mountains. You have that power to make the mountains move just as Elijah's prayer stopped the rain for three years. It's the same Spirit that lives in you.

Death Cannot Hold Us Down

The more we grow in Christ, the less we should be afraid of death. I believe God wants us to know we belong to Him, and as we trust in who He is, we receive His perfect peace when it's our time to go. When we do not think in alignment with God, we are subjected to bondage. For the love of God casts out all fear.[43] The opposite of love is fear.

---

43   1 John 4:18

Paulo Freire, a Brazilian expert on education has stated, "The opposite of love is not, as we many times or almost always think, hatred, but the fear to love, and fear to love is the fear of being free." When we are fearful, we are operating outside of God's purposes for our lives, even in the way we think about death. Since we are children of God of flesh and blood, He too, shared in our humanity so that by His death He would break the power of him who holds the power of death, that is, the devil. He releases all those who through fear of death were all subject to bondage all their lifetime.[44] Therefore, when we draw closer to Him, fear will be broken because, in His presence, there is peace and love.

We are able to control our fears, and it is our choice to accept God's word or accept the way we feel. When a young friend/child or a new Christian passes on to be with the Lord, and it seems as though they died too soon as a devout or new Christian, we can remember Isaiah 57:1. It states, "The righteous perish, and no one takes it to heart; the devout are taken away, and no one understands that the righteous are taken away to be spared from evil." We have no idea what evil might be ahead for them, but God loves us so much that He will protect our souls to not go back to the devil where we may not be able to come back to Him. Jesus says:

"I give them eternal life, and they shall never perish; no one will snatch them out of my hand. My Father, who has given them to me, is greater than all; no one can snatch them out of my Father's hand."
John 10:28-29

---

44   Hebrews 2:14 paraphrased

I remember my grandfather had a hard, couple of last years in his life; it was a humbling experience for him to be bedridden and taken care of by his children. A couple of days before his death, he told my mom, "Jesus saved me." God is so faithful, even on our last breath. That is how merciful our Father is.

"Precious in the sight of the Lord is the death of His saints."[45] When believers die, God considers it precious, literally, and figuratively. What do you think of as valuable? Consider Jesus seeing you as precious in His sight. What do you think of when you hear that? Do you believe it? Whether we live or die we belong to the Lord.[46] We cannot assume we know what God is thinking when He takes a loved one "home," but we must choose to believe it is ultimately for their good. Death is not something we should be afraid of, especially when we believe in our Lord Jesus Christ. We are not to fear those that can kill the body and are not able to kill the soul, but rather to fear God who can destroy both soul and body in hell.[47]

Fear is a spirit. There are many things that can "feed" this spirit if we allow it. Thinking about doubt and entertaining the thoughts of hopelessness, feeds this spirit. To not feed the fear, we choose instead, to believe that God wants us to live in Spirit and truth. He created for us a pathway to eternal life with Him. God truly has given us a spirit that has conquered death's meaning. To keep our focus on what is eternal, not just the present, we think about all that He has done for us. We do not belong to the spirit of fear, but the spirit of power, love, and a sound mind.[48] We keep God's power as our focus in what He has accomplished through Jesus, who defeated the

45   Psalm 116:15
46   Romans 14:8
47   Matthew 10:28
48   2 Timothy 1:7

grave. Jesus came to give us life and to live it more abundantly, in the physical and spiritual.

Our thinking must align with God's word if we want His results in our lives. To overcome any wrongful thinking, iniquities, bondage, and strongholds in our lives, we must release all our fears and fully surrender. The fear of death is a stronghold, a lie, and bondage. He did not come, so we would be fearful of dying. He came so we can defeat death. When we die, our spirit leaves our bodies to be with the Lord. That means our soul does not sleep. Instead, we immediately are ushered into the presence of the Lord. With a twinkling of an eye, we move into His glorious kingdom. So, whether we die or live, we belong to Him,[49] moving from glory to glory. In the book of Revelation, it states:

> *"He who overcomes I will give him these things (wipe every tear, no more death, no mourning, nor crying nor pain, and freely drinking from the spring of life), I will be his God and he will be my son. But for the cowardly, unbelieving, sinners, abominable, murderers, sexually immoral, sorcerers, idolaters, and all liars, they will part in the lake that burns with fire and sulfur, which is the second death."*
> Revelation 21:7-8

People will die twice. Ouch. The second time they will be in that place forever; hell is eternal separation from God. That is why being obedient to God is so important. When we obey, we will defeat death. When we do life our way, we are not being obedient but making a choice to go to hell. Knowing He is the very breath of our

---

49   2 Corinthians 5

being should give us the courage even to face those who persecute us, knowing to whom we belong. As believers, we have not only died with Him but are raised with Him and seated with Him in the heavenly places.[50]

Prayer is Important

Prayer replaces our doubts, fears, negative thoughts, and low self-worth with the possibilities of what God can do. It invites heaven to release the angels to move on our behalf, tearing down the strongholds against our loved ones and fighting our battles in the unseen realm. It states our battles are not against flesh and blood but darkness and principalities.[51] To some, it may not make sense. Why doesn't God make people believe, and why doesn't He save everyone? *Why* do I have to pray for God to do something? Shouldn't God do that *if* He is a loving Father?

Imagine a father giving you everything you could ever want.
As though there were no limits to saying "no."
Imagine having everything you could dream of, instantly.
Now ponder on the question:
Do you think you would appreciate things more
if your father did not give you everything
you ever wanted and if you fought (in prayer) a little more
to get what you wanted? Do you think you would value
what you received a little more if you waited?
I did not get everything I wanted.

50   Ephesians 2:6
51   Ephesians 6:10

In fact, at 11 years old, I started my first job
because my mother would complain about money
not growing on trees. Because I started working young,
I knew what it meant to work hard
and learned that if I wanted to get anything in life,
I needed to be the one to make it happen.

However, in the home, I use to think that God
had forgotten me, because many times, I did not feel loved.
My parents would argue, and my dad would be consumed
with the television. At times, he would leave to go to the bar,
which made it seem like he would try not to be at home.

My mother would always yell, criticize and take her frustration
out on my older brother and I.
My mother would say comments like,
"Boys do this and girls do that,"
so it caused division in the home.
Her words hurt me, calling me stupid, fat, and ugly.

There was even a time when I did not think she knew my name
because for a long time I didn't hear her say, "Eva."
She would call me, "Girl." My friends eventually caught on,
mocked her, and made fun of me for it.
I would laugh it off, but deep down, it hurt me.
There was no thought or love in the statement, *girl*.
Anyone could be "girl." It was so impersonal to me.
I didn't feel like I fit in anywhere.
I would often get made fun of at school.
I felt alone a lot.

Then my parents got divorced.

I remember praying to God and
asking Him to put me into a new family
because obviously, He forgot about me.
I didn't quite understand why He would not
miraculously put me into a new family,
with new friends, in a new neighborhood.
I mean, He is God, and if He can do anything,
why wouldn't He answer my prayer?
Why would He let me go through so much hurt and pain?
Did He not care about what I was going through?
Is it because He is too busy doing everything else?
I thought maybe it's because
I don't matter to Him.

Ever have these thoughts? It is easy not to understand God and become mad at Him because we do not know what He is doing. We think we know how things should be or think things should go our way. We sum up our pain and hurt as though God has no idea what we are dealing with or if He does, He is cruel not to intercede and help. Being angry at God is normal. Anger is a normal emotion that we all go through. However, when we are mad, it normally makes us turn from God rather than go to Him. We are either becoming bitter or better.

Better means humbling ourselves and praying for God to intercede. *Better* means releasing our hurt and pain and relying on God to comfort us. *Better* means trusting God, even when we do not understand. It's much easier to become bitter. Too often, we think we know what is best for us, and in turn, we become our god. We do what we want, when we want and ignore the fact that God is with us all the time. We may instead take control, do things our way, hoping to not go through any hurt or experience pain (again). And in this process, we learn to manipulate others and think we need to protect ourselves our way, whether it is not letting people get close or only surrounding ourselves with certain types of people. We tend to believe that if God is loving, there shouldn't be any pain. But sadly, that isn't so. In life, we will experience pain. In Christ, we learn how to get through it with Him. In heaven, there is no sickness, disease, or distress, but here on earth, we experience heartache, suffering, and destruction. Our hope as believers is knowing heaven is preparing for Christ's coming, and what we suffer or endure here, will not compare to the joy that is set before us.

Even though I was raised Catholic,
I knew *about* Jesus but believed He was far from me.
I didn't understand why I would have to go
to a priest to confess my sins
if I could talk to Him anywhere?
I stopped going to church.
Soon after, so did my mother.

Feeling as though God was far from me,
I distanced myself from Him. I took *life* into my own hands,
hardening my heart from people to not get hurt again.
In high school, my mother and I would argue so much
I decided to stay with my boyfriend at his parents' house
but still felt the struggle of being misunderstood
in all areas of my life. The only thing consistent
in my life was holding a job.

I worked at Arby's for eight years, and I was a manager.
I loved hiring and training my crew;
it felt more like *home* than anything else.
But something was still missing.
I wasn't satisfied with who I was as a person.

Smoking cigarettes, drinking alcohol and
dishonoring my body did not satisfy me.
I still felt *empty.* I realized I wasn't *in love*
with my boyfriend and broke it off with him.
I met someone else and quickly jumped
into the relationship because
I didn't like the feeling of being alone, plus,
I needed a place to go other than my mom's house.

Three months after we dated,
he told me he had a child on the way.
I wasn't as upset about the child,
as I was about him lying about it.
Holding something from someone is still lying to them.
But I brushed it off and tried to work with it.
But then, my great grandmother, Emilia passed away.

Her death was hard for me.
When I would visit with her,
she would always tell me, "You're pretty."
This made me feel special.
She didn't speak much English,
but she would always repeat those words to me.
It was as though a piece of me went with her
because I had nobody else in my family telling me
that I was *pretty*, which spoke to me as though *I mattered.*

Because my boyfriend was not able to be there for me
during a crucial time in my life
and lied about what he was doing, we broke up.
Our breakup forced me to go back to my mother's house.
Six months after we broke up, I was asked if I wanted
to try cocaine and I found no reason not to.

I said to myself, "Why not? They already see me this way."
It consumed my life for three years.
For three years, I was high.
High on whatever I could get my hands on.
I've tried and done it all. I lived from house to house,
staying anywhere that someone would accept me.
I felt hopeless, unwanted, used, and abused.
When I think of a time in my life
that was shameful and regretful, this was it.

There was one person in my life
who told me I mattered, my best friend, Jon.
He kept telling me how Jesus loved me
and had great plans for me,
and we would often get into arguments
because I truly believed God didn't *know* me.
I mean *obviously* how could God care about me?
I thought, "If He *really loves* me,
my life would look much different from *this*."

I compared His love to my circumstances.
My best friend Jon was persistent in calling me.
I would tell him *everything* because, *well*,
he was in prison.
I figured he wouldn't judge me

based on what he had done.
But throughout the time of us talking,
I quickly realized he saw life differently than I did.
Something enabled him to think he could keep *going.*
I was in an overdose state when I saw in a vision.
My life before me. I was in a coma state,
laying down on a hospital bed,
with my parents looking down on me,
asking me, "How could *you* have done this to yourself?"
I was so mad, and all I wanted to say was,
"You guys did this to me!"

But it was at that moment that I realized,
I was making all my decisions, *myself.*
My parents were not *making me* make my choices.
I made my own choices. It was how I chose to react.
I wasn't *just* blaming my parents.
I was blaming God.
But how often do we blame others for our actions?
It's as though we all of a sudden have no option but
to rebel or act out in our hurt or pain.
"I have that right," we tell ourselves.

We Choose Our Attitudes

"Attitude is a product of belief."
- Myles Munroe

Attitudes are patterns of thinking and these patterns have been with
us since childhood. Mine was to blame others for what happened to

me. Ultimately, I was blaming God, and, in a sense, my "self" became revengeful. We go into attack mode for survival when we do not feel safe or protected, and we end up self-sabotaging our potential for greatness. We settle for mediocre because it's what we do to *keep ourselves* secure. We settle for thinking we need to retaliate, *we need* to take care of ourselves, or *we must do something* rather than depending on any "god" to make it happen. We switch to protect ourselves, and in a way, we become our own "god."

I wonder if it was God who wants us not to *settle*, and who allows us to get tired of being *sick and tired?* Has He been all along cheering for us to do something *different?* We all have free will. We all have free choice. Sometimes we don't realize that when we don't do something about a concern or situation, we are still choosing to do *something*, even if it is *nothing*. We are choosing to stay in that disappointment or however it may be making us feel. We can give our power away, thinking we cannot do anything, or we keep our power by choosing to have something important and worthy for in our lives, comfort and mediocracy over pain and suffering. In the battles, our true *greatness* gets diminished because we do not know who we are. And soon enough we blend in with everyone else, not *being* the salt or the light that Jesus says that we are because we haven't learned how to fight for ourselves and stand up for who we are as *children* of God.

How can we be *set apart* if we look and sound
like the rest of the world?
Where is our *flavor* that the world needs?

Hidden. Tarnished. Bewildered.
Is *this* the life Jesus died for us to have?
Where is the abundance that He promises?
Did He *lie?*

For we know, God does not lie, for no evil comes from Him. Yet, we act like He isn't telling the truth because we resort to our ways, thoughts, and actions. So, being Christian now looks fake to unbelievers when we are not standing up to whom God says we are. Many people call themselves Christians, yet there are so many definitions to being one. It's almost humorous to think that we have to ask each other, "What kind of a Christian are you?" We are all not the same, yet God calls us to be unified. To be united, we meet and serve people where they are, not trying to be better than others, but humbling ourselves when others are weak, and asking more questions to get to know people.

Give Grace and Mercy to Others

There are far too many divisions between us, but our lives are to represent our Father, yet we can't even get along with those in our households. How can we ever live unified if we are too busy thinking about ourselves *(my needs, my wants, my desires)*? Would we rather cut people out of our lives or hold an offense rather than try to get along with them? Do we try to understand other people and their perspective? Are we mindful about giving them grace in a matter *(argument or circumstance)* or show empathy *(understanding or concern)* for what they are going through?

I have fallen into protecting myself too many times as well, tending to cut people out of my life rather than explaining how I may be feeling. However, recently, I have been trying something new where I allow myself to be vulnerable with people. I let them into my heart and share my thoughts and opinions. I talk about my insecurities with them, giving them the opportunity to decide if they want a relationship with me. I don't try to force myself into a relationship with people anymore. I let them know I'm thinking about them and let them know I'm always here if they need me. Then, I let it *be*. "Above all else, guard your heart, for everything you do flows from it."[52]

Guarding our hearts is protecting them from building offenses. I have removed some people from my Facebook to set up boundaries. I must protect myself from taking an offense, comparing myself, or anything that is not good for my eyes to see or ears to hear. With everything being on social media nowadays, it's hard not to post about what's happening in our lives. But what is the real motive behind these posts? Are they intended to make others jealous, to passive-aggressively get someone back, to gossip, or compare? For God to be pleased, we are to do all things unto Him, and that means even our social media posts! Our social media is our platform to praise God in public.

We get to show the world who we belong to and who we believe in. We get to share our testimonies, joys, strengths, and weaknesses. But what a shame to be a Christian in secret where it is hidden or to represent our Father as though we have no reverence for Him. For no one to know that You are a child of God, when the world is

---

52   Proverbs 4:23

in desperate need of you, does not show how much you love your Father, or show how much He loves you.

Are you aware of how much He loves you?
Are you fully convinced of His love for you?

We have something that the world needs, and that is Jesus, who resides inside of His children. But if we don't understand who He is, we will never produce results or fruit in and through our lives. We must genuinely surrender and give Him *all* of us. We can say we are *all in* for Jesus, but what we actively practice will show if we truly serve the Lord. What we believe *in* will dictate what we say and do. What we think will be manifested in our words and actions. To represent Jesus, we follow Him even when our feelings don't align with the truth of God's word. That is obedience.

Jesus was Obedient to Death on the Cross

Jesus didn't talk about how others made him feel. He focused on His Father and asked Him to take death from Him if it was His will, but He wanted to accomplish His will even if it meant being beaten, bruised, suffering persecution, and dying on a cross. So often we do not make amends or forgive because of what others have said or done to us. Yet, Jesus said to forgive someone seven times 70; it's endless. For all things, we should forgive and if we find ourselves easily angered, we can put into practice forgiving quickly, so our anger doesn't build up. I purposefully say out loud, "I choose to forgive (specific name)," even though I don't feel like it. I turn it into a joke and laugh at it because I can quickly get angry over the "small" things. I try to make light of it and laugh at myself because laughter has a way of brightening our days even when our days are hard. To live above our feelings, means changing something small (like adding laughter).

Our brains can shift into something new which enables our attitudes to improve. It's changing what we would typically do, to something that may not make sense to us because we are doing it in faith. This will help us change our feeling to align with what we want to think according to God's holy ways. Many of us may want to think good thoughts towards those who do us wrong, so we must learn how to love ourselves enough in the process. This way we can genuinely love the person back who may have offended us. When we think about Jesus and the cross, we are to remember that He was not looking forward to the chastening but had hope for what was to come. He was thinking about us. Everyone who enters our lives have an opportunity to meet Jesus through our love. When people hurt us, it's an opportunity to show who He is and what He has done for us. This will allow God to work in their hearts.

Throughout my life, I have struggled with depression.
Some days have been challenging for me
to get out of bed and feel excited about life.
Many times I have not had the motivation
to keep moving forward, in fact,
I have cried out to God to help me
throughout my day because
I have felt so alone in my despair and heartache.
I've had thoughts of giving up the fight.

I have tried to believe that there
is hope in the battlefield.
So to move forward, I decide to focus
on one day at a time and try not to get
overwhelmed with life's complications.

Hope deferred makes the heart sick (Proverbs 13:12), which means, when we do not have hope, we can become physically immobilized. Lack of hope stops us from moving forward because if we sit there too long, we start allowing the feelings of defeat to take over.

It has been my internal battle that makes me think,
how can I ever be good enough?
But God, by His grace and mercy,
doesn't base things on my failures or my past,
but by His goodness, He helps me to
fight through and persevere.
Setting my eyes on God helps me
to overcome my emotions,
knowing He is faithful,
He cannot deny Himself.

You have something that the body of Christ needs, and that is your gifts and talents that God gave you. You will never find out what those are if you exclude yourself from others. You can be all God has called you to be because He equips the called and will bring it to completion. God is not done with anyone who still has breath in them. God has a purpose and plan for everyone. It is not easy, but it becomes worth it. Learning to die to yourself every day is a process. Learning how to be unselfish can be exhausting, due to the fact when you meet other people's needs, you give up something you may potentially want to do at that time. God has given us His Spirit, to lead us, guide us, and counsel us to His righteousness and holiness.

Right after I came to Las Vegas,
I knew I was here for God,
but I didn't want to go to church.
All I knew was the Catholic Church,
and it felt empty and unsecured.
I didn't understand why I should tell
my sins to a priest when I could talk
to God Himself?

I started going to the mountains
to pray and build my relationship with Jesus.
Until my battle became too much for me to handle alone,
I knew I needed help, which lead me to a church.
I'm so thankful someone told me about
Central Christian Church.
Without this person being persistent
and inviting me to church,
I would not have known which church to go to
and would have continued in my strength
to fight my temptations.
Going to the church provided me
an opportunity to be prayed for
and because of someone else's gift,
I was able to receive what God was doing:

healing me from my past
and providing me with a church family.

No temptation has overtaken you except what is common to mankind. God is faithful; he will not let you be tempted beyond what you can bear. But when you are tempted, he will also provide a way out so that you can endure it.
1 Corinthians 10:13

Submitting ourselves to do what we don't want to do will produce a good outcome when it's according to God's will. When we come together in the house of God, we can advise one another in our faith to keep doing the good work which He calls us to do by the Holy Spirit who witnesses to us. We can hold fast to His promises of putting His laws into our hearts and minds, as He chooses not to remember our sins and lawless deeds anymore. It is His promise that He has given to us.

Now that we live through the consecration of Jesus Christ through His flesh, we can enter into His presence with boldness and assurance as to our High Priest. He accepts us as we draw near with a pure heart in full assurance of faith, having our hearts sprinkled from an evil conscience (of the mind) and our bodies washed with pure water. Let us hold fast the confession of our hope without wavering, for He who promised is faithful.
Hebrews 10 19-23

If we are honest, it is easy to fluctuate, but He who has called us can accomplish more than we can think or imagine. We must learn to move toward Him rather than disconnect, by doing what we think is best.

It's lovely to celebrate others, but so often we don't. We get jealous and compare ourselves to what others are doing. Comparison steals our joy. Comparison makes us focus on what we are lacking rather than what we could be doing. We talk about where we should be and what we should have. Talking about the "what if's" or "should have's" disable us from moving forward because thinking this way keeps us in negative thinking, discouraging us from wanting to do anything. We will stay in our same cycle. We think complaining will somehow motivate us to do something different, but it never does. We waste our time by complaining, blaming, and gossiping about what we like or don't like or what is fair and what isn't. For our behaviors to shift into a new cycle of interaction, we have to keep our focus on God. Seek first the kingdom and His righteousness and everything else will be added unto you.[53] When we focus on His kingdom and righteousness, we become faithful in our walk with Him.

Focus on God

When I started praying for my husband, I was focused on God. I was getting ready to speak at my first conference and deliver a message God put on my heart. I was reading the Bible every day. I listened to Christian music on Pandora and soaked in it. Singing is a form of praise, and it keeps our hearts fixated on God. There is also a term called *soaking*, which I would do at least twice a week. I put on music

---

53   Matthew 6:33

and meditated on the words of God's goodness with my eyes closed, believing what I was hearing is true, and allowing the words to penetrate my heart. When this happens, my spirit gets accelerated in His presence because it's all about Him and His truth. It's a form of meditation and brings me closer to our Father.

Meditation should be done with our minds focused on God. We should be filling ourselves up with more of Him and releasing all our cares and worries to Him. We should not be emptying ourselves, but rather, meditating on His words that fill us with hope and trust in Him. The more we read the Bible, the more we think His thoughts, the more we will be able to conquer the battles in our minds. We all have battles and in them we must choose which voice we will listen to. The voices that bring us self-doubt, condemnation, shame, or guilt are not of God. God will correct you, encourage you, convict you, and lead you to do things that will strengthen your character. God's ways are not our ways, and so often we think that if we are not comfortable with something, then it must not come from God. We think God wants us happy and comfortable. We might think if it doesn't feel right, then it must not be from God. But God doesn't base things on whether we will be happy about it or if things *feel* right. He does things based on *His pleasure.*

God Wants Us Happy, but that Doesn't Mean We'll *Always* be Happy

God cannot make us *all* happy, *all* at the same time. He made us uniquely different so some will be happy, and others will not be, given the situation or circumstances. Even when we are being corrected to know God's ways, the Bible considers we shall be happy.[54] We are

---

54   Job 5:17

happy when we find wisdom and gain understanding, not just when we find a spouse or get a job.[55] Although, this may be good for us, it does not produce the *rightful happiness* God requires for us. He who heeds the word wisely will find good and whoever trusts in the Lord, happy is he.[56] You are worth being happy, but to a Christian, it looks different than how the world perceives it. For righteousness sake, you shall be happy. This promise ultimately gives us contentment because we are putting God's Word into our hearts. Seeking the Kingdom of God is finding out what we are to possess to enter His Kingdom.

Not everyone who worships the Lord will be entering into the Kingdom. Jesus said, "Many will seek to enter and will not able."[57] Workers of iniquity *(unfairness, immoral, and wicked behavior)* will not enter the Kingdom. If immoral people were to enter heaven, there would be no reason to pray, "...on earth as it is in heaven" because heaven would look like earth. However, since we pray, "...on earth as it is in heaven," we know there is no immoral, wicked, or unfair behavior in heaven. Because heaven is holy, and there is no evil thing in heaven, we must believe that God cares about what enters into His Kingdom. That is why not all good people will go to heaven. It is not based on being *good,* instead, it is based on who you *believe*, God, or the enemy.

There is a Spiritual Battle with Our Identity

There is an unseen realm in which we are fighting. We may think that we are fighting against a person we are in conflict with because

---

55   Proverbs 3:13
56   Proverbs 16:20
57   Luke 13:24

that is what we see and that is what we can acknowledge (the person is upsetting us), but faith is the thing we cannot see. It is the spiritual battle working against us. The enemy roams around like a roaring lion, looking to see whom he can devour.[58] This is not our playground, but the enemy's. However, God has given us a mandate to rule on earth, in which, knowing our position, we can rule, but only if we know *who* we are battling. We are not fighting each other, but we think we are because of what other people say and do. Our battles are not against flesh and blood, but darkness and principalities.[59] Since it is by faith that we believe Jesus is risen, then it is by faith that we believe there is a spiritual world that is not seen.

The enemy has studied mankind since the beginning of time, and his tactics are *not* new. We have to know the battle starts in our minds. The enemy will have us doubt God's love for us, and he will try to convince us we lack something good. He will shame us or put guilt on us, and we might compare ourselves to others. He will have us believe we have to blame others or have us become more prideful in who we are or covet what we own. Often, he wants us to think nobody likes us or that we are alone in the battles.

These are his tactics, but God has not made us in his likeness. You were made in God's image. To know who He is, is powerful. We can come to understand the power we have on the inside of us and the ability to create just like our Heavenly Father creates with His words and work. We are His workmanship. It is by faith that we can create, but only if we choose to look for the possibilities rather than the problems. The enemy has a God-given purpose on earth, and it *could be* to help us stay in our rightful position as heirs with God

58   1 Peter 5:8
59   Ephesians 6:12

when conflict comes. In the conflict, we grow and become refined in God's likeness. Just like a diamond gets formed out of pressure, so do we. Pressure comes from people, circumstances, and choices. When we focus on God, our desires shift to what is important to Him, which most likely, may cause friction *within*.

Where There is Fire, There is Growth

Many times, we do not face the fire, and we go back to our self-protected ways to keep ourselves safe and satisfied. We want to believe that if God is good, then nothing wrong should ever happen to us, but this is an unrealistic expectation of God. God allows terrible things to happen all the time because of free will. He doesn't want robots following Him; He wants hearts set out for Him. If God didn't want the enemy roaming the earth, then he would be bound up already, but since God has a purpose to use him in our lives, we must know what we possess, which is the key to the Kingdom. Our faith enables us to overcome the tactics of the enemy and sets us where Jesus is seated, as an heir.

If you do not know how you are positioned, how do you think you can rule? Rising above our circumstances involves taking our seated position in Christ. God knows what will come our way, how it will come to us, and why it will happen. We then will have a choice in our attitude and can decide what to do. We will always have a choice. Our power is not to be freely given away to manipulators, controllers, or abusers. We must know who we are to stand firm in our faith and be able to move forward. It starts with identity.

We will probably not have a clear picture of our heavenly Father, if we had an earthly dad who abused *(mentally, emotionally, physically, or sexually)* or rejected us or was absent in our lives. We can have a distorted image of Jesus if friends or family have back stabbed us or rejected us. We can misunderstand how to surrender the need of control if we have had a controlling or abusive mother. We all can have a mis-perception of God, Jesus, and the Holy Spirit based on our relationships and experiences. To have a healthy relationship and be in unity in our faith with other Christians, we must have the right image of our Heavenly Father, Jesus, and the Holy Spirit. Otherwise, we will continue to walk around, hurting others because we do not understand who we are representing. To be attractive to the world (the world will know us by our *love*), we must learn God's attitudes through Jesus and submit our thoughts to His thoughts.

Attitude of Grace

When we think about what the Lord has given to us: grace and mercy, we too can give grace to others who don't deserve it. Grace is extending peace in a situation. It offers allowances for what has happened. Anger and strife only intensify pridefulness. They do not produce the character of God, although anger can come from God, and He does get angry. However, He is also slow to anger. Lowering our expectations for others may be the first thing we do in our relationships to keep us from building up anger or receiving offenses.

When we expect something from others, like unspoken rules in our minds, it may build up resentment and criticism when people fail to meet our expectations. These may stem from our past and the way we were raised. We learned early in life how to get our way, what we should or should not say, and how to act and behave. We developed earthly mindsets to keep us safe from experiencing pain. We may have put up walls and created unhealthy relationships and behaviors, which can affect how we communicate.

Imagine a passive person *(someone who withdraws from arguments or does not address issues)* and an aggressive person *(someone who overtly states their opinion with their words and/or behavior)*. Picture the aggressive person getting upset because something was not put away properly in the home or something wasn't done right at work. The passive person may not understand the reason for the anger but sees the person upset and thinks to themselves, "This person is crazy." It can look crazy to a person, who does not normally react this way, but instead of asking questions or trying to understand, the passive person decides to withdraw from the situation. He or she doesn't want anything to do with someone being angry. But a withdrawn person or someone who likes to stay away from confrontation or arguments may not necessarily react the right way, *either.*

Everyone Communicates Something

Someone who expresses anger more abruptly may not be happy inside. You can see in their behavior something is not right. Withdrawn people are more likely to be passive-aggressive because they do not express what they need, but instead, take revenge on others who they consider to be "wrong" in the first place. They may say in their hearts, "I don't want to hang out with this person," or they may talk about what someone did to them and why it was their fault, without ever confronting or talking to the person.

Whether we react or respond, we have within embedded deep *truths* about ourselves. For aggressive people, it may be that they are trying to get their voice heard and are more "dramatic" to get their messages across and are unaware of how to express them in a calm manner. Perhaps, they were never taught how to use their words. For passive people, they may have learned that their words don't matter, so they decide to stay silent because it is comfortable for them. No matter what we have believed as our inner truth, these are the seeds of "deception" and they are not who we really are. Yet, we communicate as if others know our expectations. However, they don't. We all are saying our 'truth' to what we believe about ourselves and others in some way, whether we realize it or not. What we have experienced creates our perceptions. Our perceptions can always change if we decide to gather more information about the situations and the people involved, instead of placing judgments on them.

Childhood Beliefs

There are things that we believe about ourselves that we picked up from our childhood. We all have beliefs about who we are and what we can do or accomplish. Chances are they are more harmful than we care to admit. If you honestly looked in the mirror and said all your thoughts about yourself out loud, would you be pleased with them? Probably not. We can be our worst enemy. I wonder why that is? Why don't we love ourselves without having to feel puffed up as though we are something we're not? Why don't we really love ourselves as if we mattered and have a purpose? Sometimes, we can encourage other people more than ourselves, but what if we valued who we are and encouraged ourselves just as much? I have learned that in life, I must be my best cheerleader. People have disappointments, and they may not know what you may need. So, we must be good to ourselves and love ourselves.

We cannot love others correctly if we are negating our first priority, which is to love God. Loving God enables us to love ourselves because discovering His truth shows us who we are. As believers, we believe He made us, then we too, can accept His love for us and love ourselves like He loves us. This doesn't happen without understanding who God is. We cannot have a mindset thinking God doesn't care about us, or think He is far from us or that He is too busy to be with us. For the Bible tells us that God is with us, and He will never leave nor forsake us.

How many of us act as though He can hear, see, touch, and feel everything we do? He experiences things through us. Remember how Abraham was sacrificing his only son? God was able to know how much Abraham believed in Him by his faith in action. God has feelings. Our feelings come from Him, but we may not know how to steward them rightfully or heavenly. Being led by the Spirit takes time, practice, and sacrifice. Sacrifice because it requires a commitment that we may not want to willfully do. Practice because it might seem fake to us, and it takes time because anything worth fighting for, takes a process to achieve. Listening is key when we love others.

Saying things immediately may not show that we are listening to the speaker, but instead, we can be reacting out of anxiety or fear because of our own insecurity. Self-examination helps us become good listeners to know why we react the way we do and if there is another way to respond in a matter. When we are talking with others, we can quickly be trying to think of a response rather than listening to the talker.

Instead, of trying to think of a response, we want to learn to listen to the heart of the matter so we can understand what the person is saying. To become better listeners, we need to ask ourselves, "What are they really trying to say? What are the concerns that are bothering them? What are they really trying to get across and express in so many words?" This is where asking more questions is helpful. Then, you will know how to respond rather than joining in with complaints or negativity.

Gain More Significant Clarity

A great way to gain more significant clarity is by asking people, "Do you want me to *fix it, just listen, or help you find a solution?*" By asking this question, you will learn how to respond and grow deeper in your relationships. Being purposeful in our speech and the way we communicate assures we are speaking life into people and situations.

Jesus did not use all His authority on the earth. He humbled Himself to meet people where we were, discerning the hearts of men, knowing if what He had to say would be impactful or not. The purpose was to bring a change to people's thinking and hearts. To love someone is not sugar coating the truth. Love is knowing people well enough and being able to discern if what we have to say will help them think differently and reconcile to God.

To speak with love and truth takes discernment, to know how to approach the thoughts of man. Just because someone may have the *authority*, doesn't mean they have the *power* to back up the authority. The power comes from the Holy Spirit, but if we do not know how the Holy Spirit works, we can simply misuse the gift Jesus gave us by not allowing the Holy Spirit to move in our lives. The Holy Spirit is our Counselor, leading us to all truth and excellence. He is able to reveal what the Father is doing through the scriptures and He inclines our ears to hear our Father. He is our direct link to our Father so we may know what He is doing. Many times, when we think about the Holy Spirit, we may not think of Him as a person. Since we cannot see Him, we can misunderstand who He is to us. He is our Helper, who will bring things to our remembrance of what we learned about Jesus and will teach us *all* things.[60] Jesus is our advocate, and we cannot do anything apart from Him. He fights on our behalf, going to the Father *for* us. He constantly intercedes for us and prays for us. Knowing that Jesus and the Holy Spirit pray for us, how much more important is it for us to pray for one another?

I can be so much in my own mind or head that I do not pray for people because of my own fear of what to say or concern about what others may think when I do pray, but power comes through prayer. God moves on prayer. We might see attitudes in people that are not right, and talk about them, which does not help the situation. Rather, we should be praying for them. Gossiping about others does not help but causes more tension among friends because gossip sows seeds of discord. This brings division and only puffs up egos. Even when we are listening to others, we can ask God, "What do you want me to say concerning this?" This will help us to work with

---

60   John 14:26

God and what He wants to do in any given situation. It is especially helpful to pray when we are bothered.

Always Pray, Even When It's Hard to Pray

When others make fun of us, treat us wrong, steal from us, or lie to us, we ought to pray for them. We may not want to, but it is God's desire for us to pray when we feel mistreated. Unfortunately, I have had friends who have stolen from me, talked bad about me, and used me. It's amazing to see God fight our battles when we pray. We literally do not have to respond to people but bring the situation to God in prayer. He will show us who He is when we do this. Some revelation happens right away, but others take some time. No matter the time, God always hears our prayers. Believe in your heart that you matter to Him, especially when someone treats you wrongfully. Forgiveness doesn't give people excuses for what they did, but think about how Jesus prayed on the cross, "Lord, forgive them, for they do not know what they do."

Many people give excuses and say that they know what they are doing, but chances are, deep in their hearts, they really don't. They may be doing what was taught to them, and although it does not give them an excuse, they really do not know any other way to treat people. They have never been shown how to truly love someone. People cannot learn new ways or thoughts without learning how. It won't just "come" to them unless God decides to give them revelation, but chances are, He won't. He wants us to work out what is *in* us. How do we know what is in us unless we get tired of having the same results, and we realize we do not want the negative cycle to continue?

Hurt People Hurt People

Hurt people hurt people because they don't *know* any better. To change this, people usually need to have the self-awareness that they need to change. Until this happens, they will keep being *them* because that is all they know. Many people do not want to instruct others how to act, because they feel like they *should* know. If we learn to love people, we will find that loving them comes through serving them in the area where they need help. Their attitudes and behaviors are things we can help them with, but only if we know ourselves well enough to know *why* we are helping in the first place. It should not be because of manipulation or control, but because of justice and love.

For years, I wanted to change my mother.
I wanted her to speak kindly to me
and have her ask about my day and
get to know me or want to spend time with me.
In my early years, I would blame myself
for how she treated me.
I would say, "I shouldn't have done (a, b, or c),
so she wouldn't get mad at me."
Even though I *knew* it wasn't my fault,

I wanted to make peace.
By my middle and high school years,
I was so tired of her doing the same thing
over and over again that I became distraught
and fed up with her behavior and attitude.
I spoke to her harshly.

I was rudely honest with her and to some outsiders,
I seemed like a brat of a daughter.
This continued until after my overdose state.
Until one day I realized, I couldn't change her.

Since I desired to have a relationship with her,
I realized I needed to accept her for who she is.
After learning a little bit more about
why she treated me the way she did,
I was able to forgive her and have compassion
toward her and love her for who she is,
by accepting her the way she is.
She did the best she could do for me,
even though I didn't understand
her way of love or connection.

Many of our relationships are like this. Instead of learning from people who are different than us, we assume something is wrong with them and we cut them out of our lives. We "don't have time," or reason in our minds we should not pursue the relationship. We rarely want to see things through their perspective or learn to grow in empathy towards them.

But what if we decided to fight through our insecurities and the way we feel and instead *own* what we really think? What if we accepted that they make us feel unappreciated, unimportant, and insignificant, but we don't react from how we are feeling. Instead, we choose to *own* that this is how we feel and make the decision (without being overridden by emotions) to love them anyway.

What if we thought, "It's okay that my needs are not being met." Or "What do I need to do in order for them to realize that their voice is heard?" "They matter and maybe it's not about me at all. Maybe it's about me helping them understand they are loved no matter how we may be interpreting it." Our minds can change when we can look at people and our circumstances differently if *we choose to.*

That is the Attitude of Grace

God knows what is happening to us and what is going on with the people who seems to be treating us unfairly. Obviously, when it's someone close to us, it hurts more, but that is an opportunity to go to God in our hurt rather than substances that only mask the pain for a little while. As believers we say, "God is in control. He can do anything. He can work anything out for our good." But, when it comes down to it, and something happens to us, or a family member gets sick, or our dreams gets shattered, our finances crumble, or our relationships are in conflict, we may start to think that God won't work it out *for* us.

When we get hit with bad news, we might rather complain about it, ask why, or do what is comfortable for us. We might go to other substances like drugs, alcohol, or people, rather than Jesus Christ. We might go into our own thinking patterns, and behaviors we have used in the past to make us feel safe, but it is a false security. Our minds can make us think we should have what others have or be in their position or be somewhere better than the place we are in, which creates an illusion that God doesn't love us. This distracts us from His goodness. We fail to see others the way God sees people and we fail to truly celebrate who they are in Christ because the enemy wants to keep us divided and make us think God is withholding something good *from* us. Every day we are given a choice how we live our day and whether we will have a good attitude about it. We must practice the things we want to master. Are we going to encourage someone who needs it? Cheering someone on may not come easy but that is honoring others above ourselves. God says, "Be devoted to one another in brotherly love; give preference to one another in honor."[61] Doing this daily helps us to overcome comparison and jealousy.

Loving Someone on Purpose Doesn't Happen by Mistake

Many times, we want the blessing of God, but we bring in past behaviors and past mindsets. We want what He is doing, but we think we can get what He has for us with our same old attitude. We say, "Yeah God, I want you to bless me, but if he/she doesn't treat me right, I'll kick 'em to the curb." We may still think in our terms of *trust* and being *safe*.

I wonder why God chose Mary to be the mother of Jesus. We know there is a logical connection through the bloodline, but why wasn't Mary's mother chosen or her mother's mother? In the book of Luke, Mary answered God's call with, "I am your servant."[62] She knew her identity. She knew her place and stance. When Mary said, "...behold the maidservant of the Lord," she was talking about herself. We all serve someone. Whether it's our husbands, children, jobs, homeless people, the church, relatives, or bosses. When Mary replied, "Let it be done to me according to your word," she knew God's Word was life. It was her agenda to serve the Lord to whichever capacity He

61   Romans 12:10
62   Luke 1:38

may require of her to accomplish His will on earth.

God holds His promises through His Word. God is even gracious towards us, even in our disobedience. Look at the Israelites, even today, God still protects them even though they rejected Him because they are His chosen people. Why is it unwise to reason with God? It is because you could miss out on the blessing He has for you or miss out on blessing someone else because of your *reasoning*. We see this when Jesus could not perform miracles because of their lack of faith, and that was in his hometown with his own people.[63]

They reasoned who He was and therefore had unbelief. God even let the Israelites who disobeyed Him "die-off" because of their complaining.[64] I wonder if Hannah would have complained like the Israelites, if she would have gotten blessed with a child? She was considered faithful to the Lord because she did not complain. Instead, she poured out her heart to the Lord. She realized complaining about it would not have solved anything. Instead, she went and wept before the Lord, which was the *best* decision.

So Often We Want to Blame Others

When we blame others, we are diverting any real responsibility for our choices. We can dilute the thought that we have any real responsibility by blaming others. There is no fight in us to persevere in our faith when we blame. If we truly believe God is who He says He is, then we ought to live it out in a way that our faith overrides our doubts and fears. We ought to live as though we believe God and His promises in what He can do and not rely on our own limited strength.

63   Matthew 13:38
64   Numbers 32:13

We put limits on God without realizing it. When we complain, gossip, judge, stonewall, criticize, and get defensive, we are putting things/people/circumstances in our own hands and not welcoming God into our lives for what He can do. God is not limited in what He can do because HE IS! We limit our perspective because we do not see any changes, and we tell ourselves that we have no hope for the situation or person. Instead, we must choose to believe He is able, and He is still good even when things are difficult, and we do not understand what is happening. He is in all things, which were made in and through Jesus.

Our faith can be on fire (hard to extinguish or turn off) for God when we choose to trust Him in all our circumstances. We can choose to see Him as a loving Father when He allows us and others to go through suffering, by accepting the truth that suffering produces perseverance.[65] Perseverance gives us the strength to learn how to trust Him. When we don't trust in Him, do we really believe who He says He is? We can easily look to ourselves to "fix" problems or situations, but if we don't look to Him, we are not saying, "I trust You, Lord." Instead, we are saying, "I can do this without You." *Perseverance* is being persistent in doing something despite difficulty. It is difficult to remain in faith when we do not see the help we think we need. This just leads us to stay in our own self-corrupted cycles. When we put things into our own hands, we do not trust in Jesus and the power of His resurrection.

Since Jesus came back from the dead, you in your situation be changed! You are more powerful than anything coming against you. You just have to believe His word is true and believe in your heart

---

65   Romans 5:3

that He is who He says He is. When you believe the Lord, God gives you His promise that you will not be put to shame but will receive honor.[66]

Proverbs 31 states, "Strength and honor are her clothing." These are something you can wear and are tangible. Strength comes from within us when we surrender our wants and desires to the Lord. Strength comes from pressing through the darkness in our lives to overcome the battles we face in our marriages, children, and life.

There is a strength within us only when we get down on our knees and ask for help from the One who can provide it because we cannot do it in our own strength. We can rely on our Father, who can do what we cannot do. Our total dependence is upon Him. The more we rely on Him, the more we see Him in everything we do. There is a story of Hannah in the Bible being attacked, ridiculed, and made fun of by her adversary, year after year. Yet, she said nothing. She waited until her spirit was so engulfed, she could no longer keep quiet. She poured her heart out to the Lord and He was able to open her womb and gave her a baby.

There is Power When We Wait

Think about it, when you rush and forget something, then you must rush to find what you are looking for, which results in a feeling of being rushed for the rest of the day. Nothing really works out when you rush something. Even when we cook food in the microwave it can sometimes get burned and not cook through thoroughly. God

---

66   1 Peter 2:5

does not want us to be in a hurry to say something based on how we feel or think, but rather, to cast (throw) our cares on Him. Throw how you feel to God. Let Him handle your concerns because that is what our Father does. He handles all of us.

"In the morning, O Lord, you hear my voice; in the morning, I lay my requests before you and WAIT in expectation."
Psalm 5:3

"We WAIT in hope for the Lord; He is our help and our shield."
Psalm 33:20

WAIT for the Lord and keep His way. He will exalt you to inherit the land."
Psalm 37:34

"I WAIT for you, O Lord; you will answer, O Lord my God."
Psalm 38:15

They that WAIT upon the Lord shall renew their strength; they shall mount up with wings as eagles; they shall run and not grow weary; they shall walk and not faint.
Isaiah 40:31

I think the hardest thing to do can be to wait, in any situation. I had to wait for my relationship with my mother to improve. I had to wait to get married. I had to wait for my health to get better. I have to wait to have children. We wait to get degrees, finish school, or start our careers. We wait in line at the grocery store and on the road at a stop sign or stoplight. No matter what we do, waiting is a part of life, yet we may not appreciate it or understand the process of it.

God is refining us in faith when we wait. Even when we pray and do not receive what we have asked for right away, He is growing our faith to have a burning desire to grow from within. This happens even when we face disappointments and failures. He wants us to have a zeal for Him. As you wait on the Lord, actively ask, seek, and knock. By waiting, you are putting the responsibility in God's hands, and with His guidance, He will do more through you in less amount of time than you can do in your own efforts. While we wait, we are producing longsuffering (which is patience) through His strength and understanding. As we stay connected to God through His word and fellowship with others in the faith, He is working behind the scenes, going before us to do the things we simply cannot do. Our faith gives us the courage to wait on Him in expectation, in the hope that what He promises to us will happen soon.

Attitude of Expectancy

Are you questioning whether God will fulfill your prayers? Or perhaps you are asking if you will be here to see His promise fulfilled to you and your family? Maybe you think you're too old and your time has passed. Perhaps, you don't believe God *can* use you or you feel like you don't have any gifts you can offer Him. Whatever the case may be, there are beliefs you *believe.* This is your theology.

We can easily believe that God *can* be there for us, but not necessarily that He *will* be there. Which brings me to this question: how can we receive good things if we do not expect God will give us anything? Since we are told in the Bible, "Every good and perfect gift comes from above..."[67] we must train our minds to refuse anything less than what God has already done in our lives. He has given us everything we could possibly need in our family, ministry, business, children, and so forth. The problem is that we rarely expect it.

Earlier in my faith,
I found it easier to pray for others
than myself because I didn't really believe
that I deserved anything.
In fact, this doubt still creeps up in my mind
and makes me think that I am unworthy of what I ask for.
The more we lack in our expectancy of what God can do,
the more we choose to live in fear.

When we are not expectant of God,
there is an expectation in something or someone else,
which can mistakenly take God's
sovereign place in our lives.
We can easily blame others or God
when an expectation is not met.
Having an unmet expectation makes us
doubt the goodness of God.

Many times instead of being let down,
I'd rather answer my own prayers
by not asking God at all.
But to train myself as a child of God,
I realize that my Father who *owns* it all,
wants to give me the desires of my heart
according to His will.

---

67   James 1:17

If He decides not to bless me
with what I ask for, then it is because
it is not part of His will for me
or it is not for me *right* now.
No matter the response, God always answers.

I do not let the doubt define me or
put limits on an immeasurable God.
Instead, I choose to believe
that whatever I ask from my Father
has already been given to me.
I talk about it like it's already here.
I prepare like I'm already in the position I want to be.
I position myself in my mind to be the woman of God
that He says I am, although
I may not be there yet, and
my flesh may fail me.

I do not look at what my carnal eyes see.
Instead, I decree and declare and speak
His goodness of who He says I am more than
what my mind is telling me.
Even when I was in the process of loving myself, I say,
"I'm learning how to love me."

Be truthful to how you feel.
I have not always trained myself
to be intentional about speaking *life* over myself.
When a thought is negative, I reject those thoughts,
stating, "That is not a part of me."
I have to stop those thoughts and choose
nothing less than how *He sees me*,
regardless of how I feel.
This sets me in motion to *receive* from Him.

At a prophetic conference, at the International Church of Las Vegas, a woman in their prophetic room gave me a word from the Lord. She said, "God sees you as a string of pearls." I didn't quite understand this meaning, so I went home, prayed about it, and researched what a pearl was. I found out that pearls are unique, made differently, are well-rounded, strong, rare, admirable, and valuable. The luster of a pearl refers to the glowing appearance of its surface and it is judged by its brilliance and ability to reflect light.

Our Father is the Father of Lights. Every good and perfect gift is from above, coming down from the Father of the heavenly lights, who does not change like shifting shadows.[68] This amazed me so much and I'm so thankful for this word to know how He sees me as His child. God has blessed me to see His sense of humor because exactly one year later, around the same time, I found out my husband is from Pearl, Mississippi! He certainly knows how to make me laugh! Only God could have given such a word and then backed up His word through confirmation. You can find our testimony on how God brought us together at Powerhouse Couple on YouTube. I believe from this and other great stories in the Bible, that He is the ultimate love matchmaker for His children.

Our Father really loves a good love story and even creates them, but so often we do not wait on God for our spouses. We would rather make it happen. We often tell God to bless it and then we get mad at Him when things don't work out. Eventually, we can learn how to trust God in our marriage by humbling ourselves and asking Him to make changes in our thoughts and behaviors. When we know who He is and what He has blessed us with, like Abraham and

---

68   James 1:17

Jesus, then we can be confident and make our requests known to God. We can remember the assurance of our salvation in Christ Jesus as a son or daughter and believe He will not withhold anything good for us when we are in need because He can empathize with us in our weakness, because He too, has been tempted.

Expect God to Do Miracles

Expect Him to give you the results He wants you to have. Ultimately, everything is done for His glory. Even Jesus sought to be glorified, so He may glorify His Father.[69] It is possible for our faith to grow in every season of our lives. When we are faced with trials and difficulty, they reveal what is in our hearts and what we think about God. We can expect more from God, but when we do not get it , we can be overruled by our discouragement, hopelessness, anger, and worry. Our faith enables us to align our thinking to believe God has His best intentions towards us. It enables us to believe God can bless us and even if He chooses not to. I can still be content with what I have. We can become content in whatever situation is given to us because we have put our assurance (confidence in God's ability) in Him. We know He is good no matter what the problem or circumstance is.

Sometimes, we fail to remember the reason why God blesses us and instead may *believe* it's all about us. In the midst of this kind of thinking, we can ultimately miss out on what God has for us. When our focus is off God and unto ourselves, we are no longer honoring or stewarding the gifts He has given us. This can easily become an idol in our lives. We think we know what to do, and we stop relying on God. We may get comfortable or complacent thinking we can

---

69   John 17:1

handle it our way. When this happens, there is a disconnect between God and us because God doesn't operate in anything apart from Himself. We can be saved, receive the salvation of Jesus Christ, and still not be used by Him. Fruit is not produced when we are trying to do things our way. When God blesses us with a new beginning, He will prune the things that do not belong in the new season. We can learn to be blessed by God, not just for our benefit but also for the benefit of others.

There is no blessing without responsibility. Those who are faithful and honest in small things can handle bigger blessings and responsibilities. Sometimes, we think we can obtain the blessing without having to put any work into action, or sometimes we wish the blessing is just for *us*. We may say things like, "Thanks God for my spouse. Now, I'll do with them what I want to do." We might say, "Thanks God for blessing me with my finances, but I have trips to take and things to buy." We might think, "Thanks God for my spouse and children. Now, I'll do with them what I want." Once we get the blessing, we can misuse what God has given us and forget about where our blessing came from or not even know *why* we have it in the first place. He also helps us understand it is an opportunity to give back to others, as it is written, "Therefore, as we have an opportunity, let us do good to all, especially to those who are of the household of faith."[70]

We must realize God cleanses and purifies us in faith while we endure suffering. Usually, sin, heartache, and suffering involve family, relationships, and finances. We cannot assume we will act or behave differently if our situation changes. We must learn to change

---

70   Galatians 6:10

and position ourselves ready for the blessing even when things remain the same.

> *To the pure, all things are pure, but to those who are defiled and unbelieving nothing is pure; but even their mind and conscience are defiled. They profess to know God, but in works they deny Him, being abominable, disobedient, and disqualified for every good work.*
> Titus 1:15-16

Our desire to see God working on the earth will enable us to see His miracles. We are blessed to be a blessing and to be used for His glory with what He chooses to bless us with. Since our Father is a giver, we must learn how to give as He does. So often, we cut God out of our lives when we get blessed and receive what we want. We may fail to invite God into every moment and learn what He wants to do with our blessing and gifts. This may be the same way we treat others when we feel mistreated. We may tend to cut them out of our lives when we get what we want from them (love, companionship, and security) because friction, offense, and unforgiveness *happens*.

Relationships are messy, but they are worth the fight. We cannot operate the way we use to. We cannot cut people out from our lives because of the way they treat us, even if we have been wronged. We must not retaliate or seek revenge just because we have been hurt. This does nothing for us, and only hinders what God wants to do in and through us to reach someone else who may not know the Lord. How we respond will show what we believe. If we believe our situations will not change, and decide to take matters into our own hands, we must ask, "Am I truly trusting God in this situation, and what do I need to do to trust Him?" When we understand how good God is, we can release our offenses to Him.

Represent Trust in God even when We Feel Mistreated

When our heart is breaking for others around us and the pain is too much to bear, remember our broken spirits are the sacrifices of God. He will not despise a contrite and broken heart.[71] This gives us the courage and strength to serve our Lord and Savior even when it's hard and when we are suffering. Remember, it is a promise that those who follow Him will be persecuted. All those who desire to live godly in Christ Jesus will suffer persecution.[72] We must prepare our minds to be ready to suffer in our relationships or circumstances, so we are alert and aware when it happens, so we will not be surprised by it. We prepare our minds for battle by encouraging ourselves and giving praise to God, wo we do not retaliate.

> *"If you don't live by the praises of men,*
> *you won't die by their criticisms."*
> – Bill Johnson[73]

We can easily want to please man rather than God because we want to be praised. We like it when others praise us. It makes us feel good. There were those who were afraid of the Pharisees and would not openly confess their faith for fear of being put out of the synagogue.[74] Sometimes we do not confess our faith so people will like us in our workplace, on our Facebook pages, or in our sphere

---

71   Psalm 51:17
72   2 Timothy 3:12
73   Johnson, Bill
74   John 12:42

of influence. Some would rather put up fake profiles than be real about who they are in Christ. Although, it still amazes me when people call themselves Christians, but they do not *act* like it. When we allow God to work in our hearts, we no longer have the fear of not being liked. I believe, God even removed every girlfriend from my life at one time. He was the only One I talked to after not having any girlfriends for a while. I was able to get rid of my comparison of others, my insecurities of not being liked, and my need for approval.

I had to face going through the hurt of rejection, but in that hurt, I was able to find out who I truly was, *in His eyes*. The Lord has now surrounded me with powerful women who love Him and who are like-minded in Christ. He has given me powerful prayer partners and women who love themselves enough to help others love themselves. I haven't been surrounded by jealous and malicious women in years. God has been restoring my hurt from past women's relationships through Mary Kay and many other avenues.

God is a Restorer of All Areas in our Lives

Every time someone leaves my life, I must trust that God is protecting me and I am letting go of any bitterness or resentment I may feel. I can easily get offended, so I must be mindful that God knows all things and works everything out for my good, even in my vulnerable areas. To have faith in God is to have trust in Him. You cannot move from faith to faith without trust. Just like in any relationship, having trust in the relationship takes time, commitment, and patience. To know that you can trust God is something no one can take from you. When you know you can trust Him, you experience His power working through you.

It's easy to give up on God when we do not see Him acting quickly to answer our prayer. We may get tired of waiting on Him, and think He isn't real or is too busy. We grow impatient when we feel things are not done in our time frame, but prayer isn't necessarily for God to just move on our behalf. It is for Him to change us while we wait. Being mindful of the reasons we ask things from God helps us gain self-awareness to understand if we are asking out of selfishness or personal gain. Do we really care if we glorify Him? When things are for His glory, He will do things that do not make sense to us, so no man can boast. Although, it may take time. He is always right on time.

"We have the mind of Christ."
1 Corinthians 2:16

Attitude of Repentance

Here is a prayer of repentance:

*Have mercy upon me, O God, according to Your lovingkindness; according to the multitude of Your tender mercies, **blot out** my transgressions. **Wash me** thoroughly from my iniquity, and **cleanse me** from my sin. For I acknowledge my transgressions, and my sin is always before me. **Against You, You only have I sinned**, and done this evil in Your sight-that you may be found just when You speak, and blameless when You judge.*
Psalm 51:1-4

I once read, "Sin is not meeting the commandments of God's Holy standards." When we sin, for some reason, we tend to think it doesn't matter and can think, "It's not a big deal. Everyone is doing it. This is what society is doing. I'm no different." There are many ways in which we take matters into our own hands when we knowingly hurt others to get them back, or we are hurt and feel offended. We may want others to know our pain and in response, we hurt them too. When we sin, we learn from this prayer that we are sinning against the Lord only. We are battling against God. We are behaving rebelliously (doing things in our thinking rather than doing what God would like for us to do), because it's something that we did not go to God about. We have not asked Him to intervene or asked Him for help. Being rebellious is doing something in our strength or might and not believing that God can help or will help. We have doubt or unbelief in our hearts about God. *Repentance* means *to think differently*, and *to gain a new understanding*.

When we think differently about a situation, our behavior changes. We cannot compare ourselves to the world, or even to Christians since none of us are perfect. When we look to other people, we take our eyes off the Lord. This steals our joy and makes us comfortable and complacent. Since we bring our hurts and pain from the world into the church, we need more of a relationship with God daily. Our biggest temptation may be outside of our homes if we are not girded up with His truth and mindset. We can let outside influences affect our souls and our homes. Bad company does corrupt good behavior because it's easier to do the bad than the good. Think about it, even children are not taught to sin; it comes naturally. Since doing what is bad comes naturally, we must learn how to be good.

Because Adam sinned, our flesh does not want us to do good (which is submitting to God). Our flesh wars against our spirit. We must submit ourselves to Christ to overcome the wiles of the enemy (the bad). If we continue to fulfill our fleshly desires, we will not be able to move in the spirit, for our flesh and spirit wars with each other. If we get offended and lash out, complain, control, become harsh with our words, use physical violence or spiritual manipulation, then we are acting against the spirit. We must turn from those things and flee. When we decide not to control situations and instead demonstrate peace and patience, then we are gaining self-control. We can become prideful when we do not seek godly counsel. It is written, "Blessed are those who do not walk in the counsel of the ungodly..."[75] We must remember to humble ourselves and ask for help to overcome barriers and roadblocks (stagnation and frustration) in our lives.

We have been bought with a price, and our bodies are not our own, but God's. When we choose to sin, we are sinning against our bodies. To overcome sin, we must understand why we do the things we do.

I remember it was so difficult for me
to want to stop doing drugs.
But the moment I decided
(it started in my mind)
to turn to God and made the decision
I wasn't going to get high anymore,
I fled from anything that might entice me
into taking that first step of *reasoning*, that
it would be okay, *just this one time.*

---

75   Psalm 1:1

Run Away from Things That Drive Us Further From God

We can run away from destructive cycles when we truly fear Him and grow in our relationship by understanding what it means to love what *He loves* and hate what *He hates*. We give our power over to Satan when we do not submit ourselves to Christ. We need the realization that we are not powerful enough to say *no* to our temptations. We need to be aware of any wavering we have from being *all in* to following Jesus. We can openly cry out to Him in our agony for wanting to do the right thing, confessing we are unable to do something different. When we are honest with God, He opens our eyes to see a way out of our destructive cycles.

"Whoever conceals their sins does not prosper, but the one who confesses and renounces them finds mercy."[76] Being honest with God is confessing to Him what we are dealing with internally. He knows our internal battle to be whole and complete in Him. The enemy wants us to stay in our shame and guilt by not confessing our battles from within. Not confessing our struggles to Him and others, hinders us from being healed. "Therefore confess your sins to each other and pray for each other so that you may be healed. The prayer of a righteous person is powerful and effective."[77] When we pray for others who have confessed and ask God to forgive them, God comes in agreement with what we are asking for because we are admitting our need for Him.

---

76   Proverbs 28:13
77   James 5:16

Guard Your Heart

Many times we hear the saying, "Follow your heart," but that's not what the Bible teaches. Scripture states, "The heart is deceitful who can understand it?"[78] Since following Jesus, I have learned I cannot trust my thinking, instead, I must learn how to protect my heart from making wrong choices. I must remove "outside" voices that are distracting me from the will of God. I must decide to focus on reading the Bible and speaking His truth over myself and those I love.

In our pursuit of God, we must make His voice "louder" than what people are suggesting or telling us to do if it does not align with who He is. Growing up, I did not have a close relationship with my mother, which lead to unhealthy relationships with other women. I would look to what they would say about me and try to fit into their mold, but it always backfired because I wasn't true to myself. As believers in Christ, we must learn to guard our hearts.

The definition of *guard* by Merriam-Webster is, *the act or duty of protecting or defending; it is the state of being protected, being defensively watchful and alert.* Even Jesus says to be wise as serpents and harmless as doves.[79] He is teaching we must be alert and aware of our surroundings and what is happening around us. It is having a discerning attitude. Be aware many people do not fear the Lord and can make us believe the wrong things that do not honor and serve Him. Even in the Bible, Jesus warned His disciples that they would be treated badly being delivered to councils, flogged in the synagogues, and brought before governors and kings, *as a testimony* before them and to the Gentiles.

78   Jeremiah 17:9
79   Matthew 10:16

Jesus does not guarantee we will be living a life full of happiness when we decide to follow Him. He does not promise that we will live without issues in life and that all of a sudden we will gain favor with all people and have a life of ease. Instead, He promises us that *we will be delivered into the hands who do not know Him* (but He encourages us not to worry since He will give us what to say in that hour).[80] Even in the last days, evil men and impostors will grow worse and worse, deceiving and being deceived.[81] Who are they going to fool? *Us as believers.* We must be on guard and protect our hearts and each other from sinning and doing the wrong things. Proverbs 27:5-6 states, "Open rebuke is better than secret love, faithful are the wounds of a friend, but the kisses of an enemy are deceitful."

Jesus also promises, "You will be hated by everyone because of me, but the one who stands firm to the end will be saved."[82] This is another reason why we should not boast in man, or look for approval by man, or think that someone else can affirm who we are in Christ. We cannot expect people to be excited for us when we do good things for the Lord. We cannot assume that everyone will like us, but instead, we must continue to be obedient to Christ even if what He tells us to do may look silly or sound ridiculous. Therefore, not everyone will understand the hand of God in your life. Standing firm is an attribute of salvation. When we fully surrender, repent, and walk-in obedience, *we will stand firm till the end.*

---

80 Mark 13:11
81 2 Timothy 3
82 Matthew 10:22

Attitude of Thankfulness

"Therefore by Him let us continually offer
the sacrifice of praise to God, that is,
the fruit of our lips, giving thanks to His name."
Hebrews 13:15

In all situations, have a thankful attitude. I know this may be hard. I have had difficulty being thankful in all things, but I have learned that when bad things happen to me, I choose to be thankful because I believe the Lord is working on my heart in the area I feel hurt, pain or disappointment. We continuously need to be asking, "Why am I having a bad attitude and what needs to change?" We can mistakenly think when others change, then we will feel better, or when we receive what we want, then we can have a good attitude about our situation. Even when we get blessed, we may not be ready for the blessing. We can miss out on thanking God for what He has given us and instead become bitter or ungrateful due to our lack of understanding.

Depression Can Stem from an Ungrateful Heart

When we focus on the things we do not have, it is easy to feel sad, unworthy, or lost. I have faced depression for many years, but not knowing what it was, I would cover it up with a smile. Many of my days have been filled with sadness, tears, and complaining because I didn't understand *life*. I still feel these things at times, but for the past couple of years, it has become less. Sometimes it takes me days to get back to focusing on my goals and vision for the future. I haven't completely overcome it, but it is getting better. Depression can come in many forms.

For me, depression comes as sadness. I can let discouragement and frustration with myself override any *kind* words about where I am in life. When sadness *sets in,* I usually stay there longer than I should because I would rather stay isolated. When I have this false belief, I become stuck on how to move forward. At times, I even think about God's response to Samuel, "How long are you going to mourn since I rejected him as king?"[83] It makes me think about how God knows we are mourning, but also tells us not to *stay in* it. He wants us to keep moving forward in life. The future and the unknown can be scary because we don't know what to expect. We have no idea what God has for those who love Him. "Eye has not seen, nor ear heard, neither have entered into the *heart* of man, the things which God has prepared for them that love him."[84] Notice how the scripture even says, "...*heart* of man..."

Our Hearts Precedes our Thinking

When we open our hearts (not our minds), we can receive His love for us. When you confess with your mouth, the Lord Jesus, and *believe in your heart* that God has raised Him from the dead, then you shall be saved.[85] We cannot *think* our way into being saved. Thinking does not produce salvation. It's a matter of the heart. Our hearts must be changed. "The LORD your God will circumcise your heart, and the heart of your seed, to love the LORD your God with all your heart,

---

83   1 Samuel 16:1
84   1 Corinthians 2:9
85   Romans 10:9

and with all your soul, that you may live."[86] Circumcision is that of the heart, by the Spirit.[87]

Our hearts are hardened when we compare ourselves, when we don't understand what God is doing, and when we get frustrated with relationships, family, or work. A hardened heart is not impressed with what God is doing. There are endless reasons, but that is why it is so important to ask God to soften our hearts and allow Him to change us from the inside out. To be thankful, we need our hearts changed. We can continually ask God to "soften" our hearts. It takes faith to believe God can change our hearts and for Him to move in the hearts of those we love. Instead of looking at the problem or person, try praising God for who He is as bigger, capable, and able to make the impossible *possible*.

Praise God that He can bring hope to the situation. We cannot praise Him or have thankfulness without our minds shifting our focus onto our Father. When we allow ourselves to be ungrateful, we are not demonstrating the love of our Father. Find one small thing that brings you hope and thank God for it until you can add something else to your list and keep adding something to it every day. Hope deferred makes the heart sick, so we must stay mindful of what gives us hope.[88] We can break the cycle of falling back into our disappointments when we keep our hope in Jesus.

Being intentional in thankfulness helps us overcome our need for control and keeps us content with our well-being. Our faith is activated when we are thankful in hard circumstances. It tells God,

---

86   Deuteronomy 30:6
87   Romans 2:29
88   Proverbs 13:12

"I trust You, even though I don't know what You are doing."

Attitude of Forgiveness

There is no way God can or will restore relationships in your life if you are not willing to forgive. God is not a liar when He said, "Forgive others, so that I may forgive you."[89] If we want God to forgive us, we must forgive others.

I would not be where I am today, in my relationship with my mother if I did not forgive her. Forgiving someone is not giving them an excuse for what they did, but it is learning how to *grow in compassion* for others, who may not have known any better. We cannot assume the other person knows what they are doing is wrong. When everyone acts or behaves a certain way, they really *don't know* any better. If we are not willing to look at things from their perspective, then *we are no better.*

Trying to forget, is not forgiveness. Putting it off is not forgiveness. Not trying to think about it, is not forgiveness. Forgiveness is a choice, and every day, we must choose to forgive. Over and over again, no matter what people do to us, we have to move forward. Unforgiveness hinders us from moving forward because we talk about the offense (the pain, hurt, or circumstance). It embeds strife, contention, and resentment into us when we talk about it over and over. Gossiping about it damages the hearer because you are putting your contention into his or her mind and heart. This can cause you and the hearer to become selfish and prideful. If we continue to

---

89   Matthew 6:14

seek approval from others, we are allowing ourselves to stay in our hurt rather than being healed from pain.

How Do We Move Forward?

To move forward, we have to look at why we feel mistreated, unloved, and disrespected? We may want to blame other people for their words and actions, but we need to look at ourselves and ask, "Why does this bother me?" Does the hurt stem from your childhood? Does it bring up a painful memory? Does it remind you of anything familiar? If you can think of an earlier time when the pain first began, I would like for you to close your eyes and ask God to show you where He is in the memory and then wait for what He shows you or tells you. God is always with you. We can start inviting Him into our minds to help us to move forward. When we see things from His perspective, it gives us hope and encouragement to move forward. We will be able to see Him as our Avenger. God heals. If you are not willing to allow Him to heal you of your past, you will continue to live below His purposes for you. Keep a journal and write down what you feel when going through the *Accelerate Your Faith* workbook. It gives tools for healing on your journey to becoming whole.

We can turn our complaints into praise for who God is, for our thoughts to be renewed. When we allow ourselves to complain, we ultimately complain about God, which displeases Him. Complaining is a choice just like joy is a choice. We have the power to correct our attitudes. We can fix our thinking by aligning it with God's ways. Since Jesus came to give us life, it starts with His healing from the inside out. There are two parts to healing our hearts: confessing and assurance. Confessing the sin in our lives allows us to be honest before God and gives us an opportunity to be healed when others pray for us.

When we confess our sins, "He is faithful and just and will forgive us our sins and cleanse us from all unrighteousness."[90] When we also confess our sins to one another and pray for one another, it is promised that we may be healed.[91] Our prayers, then become powerful and effective, enabling us to see God's goodness and gives us the assurance of who He is.

When we identify our emotions or feelings, they lose their power. When we have been hurt, we need to name that emotion. Anger is always the second emotion. The first emotion we feel is hurt, which stems from an insecurity, but it is usually hidden by our overt feelings of anger. When we do not express our true feelings, stating, "I felt hurt when..." then, we can give our power away to our feelings or emotions. Through life, we have learned what keeps us "safe." We can mistakenly self-sabotage ourselves by making promises to ourselves by saying, "I'll never let that happen again."

When we make these promises, we are becoming our own god by thinking we know what is best to "protect" us rather than going to God and sharing with Him our hurt or pain. When we protect ourselves, we are ultimately saying, "God, I do not trust you to protect me." When we bring (identify) our real pain to the light (or to the surface), darkness no longer has power over us. We are recognizing it and taking responsibility and authority over it, if we choose to have it no longer rule over us. We can still say, "I am mad," and have nothing change because we still want to stay in it.

90   1 John 1:9
91   James 5:16

Having an awareness of God's perspective allows us to gain peace and demonstrate power in our lives. God has given us free will, so the decisions we choose will always be a choice, even when we choose to do nothing. If we make *not doing something* our choice, we ultimately are saying, "No." We cannot understand God without going to His Son. Jesus only did what the Father did. Jesus' love was sacrificial as the Father's love is to us. It's a sacrificial love when we become obedient to Him and proclaim our faith in Jesus because we now belong to Him. Having been dead in our trespasses, we are now alive in Jesus and when we turn from our ways, we demonstrate His power in our lives. We know we could not do the new or change from the old, without Him. We are constantly changing, learning, and growing.

The enemy wants us to think that God will not love us because of our sins, but God will always love us because that is who He is. Just like parents love their children because they are theirs. Just like a parent, God disciplines those He loves. We gain understanding through our discipline. If we think we are *good* all the time, then the truth is not in us. We must recognize our Father loves us even through chastisement and discipline. He is leading, guiding and training us in the way we should go. Just because we may not have a close relationship with Him, or understand His unconditional love, this doesn't mean He doesn't know what He is doing or what we are doing. He sees and knows everything, even our deepest thoughts.

Jesus went into a town called Samaria to go get water.
While he was there, a Samaritan woman
came to the well in the middle of the day.

Jesus asked for a drink from the woman,
and surprised, she asked Him if He knew who she was?
Since the Samaritans were considered
the "bottom of the barrel," Jews did not speak to them,
especially the women. Jesus didn't directly answer
the question. He told her if she knew who He was,
she would be asking Him for living water.
She became curious and asked what do you mean
about this living water? Being a Samaritan woman,
she knew about the Jews' coming Messiah
and asked Him if He was it?[92]

The disciples did not accuse Jesus of speaking to a Samaritan woman. His character was not questioned as to why He was talking to her. This is how our character should be when others think of us. We should not assume the worse about other people, but instead, give them the benefit of the doubt. Jesus met this woman's deepest desire to be seen and known. God knew her, despite her failures. God met her where she was. He did not wait for her to pass, nor did He blame her for her sin. She also did not have to hide her sin. Being *known* gave her so much courage to go out and tell other people about Jesus because of what she heard. At that moment, she didn't care how the town people had judged her for not having a husband. She didn't care how others perceived her. She knew the God of this universe cared about her. This made her bold in her faith. Her assurance of faith motivated the Samaritans to go and check Him out. They became curious. Her testimony made the Samaritans believe in who He was because He told her all she ever did.

---

92   John 4

What if we lived a faith like this woman, where we believe God knows us? What would happen to our surroundings and people who are in contact with us? Our belief is not just for us, but for someone who needs to hear it. Our faith is a testimony for God to save someone else. Faith comes by hearing and hearing by the word of God.[93] The Samaritan woman had such a strong testimony that she told everyone, and because of this, many believed.

God approaches us from mercy. He has been merciful to us by sacrificing His Son. He will not abandon or reject us when we choose Him. When we have an attitude of forgiveness, we can let God work through us to reach those we have forgiven. Our obedience to God is an answer to someone else's prayer because they need to hear our testimony, which will give them hope for their situation. When we choose to forgive other people when they sin against us, our heavenly Father will also forgive us.[94] How much more do we need to be forgiven by our Father?

When things seem to be a mess, surrender to God and declare that God is really putting things back together. We sin daily. We speak unkindly daily. We gossip daily. We seek revenge daily. There is no good thing in us, especially when we want things *our* way. When we become a believer, it doesn't get easier, but things become more worthwhile. To keep going takes faith. God will show you new ways to overcome obstacles. We have to be mindful of our attitudes to help get us through even when it's painful, and there is uncertainty.

Be forgiving of yourself. We may make mistakes, and lack knowledge

---

93   Romans 10:17
94   Matthew 6:14

and understanding, but God keeps us by the power of His word. He knew what He was getting when He chose us, and He still accepts and loves us. Nothing can take His love from us, so we can rejoice in that truth.

Attitude of Worship

"But I will sing of Your power;
Yes, I will sing aloud of Your mercy in the morning;
For You have been my defense
And refuge in the day of my trouble.
To You, O my Strength, I will sing praises; For God is my
defense, My God of mercy."
Psalms 59:16-17

God is looking for worshippers. Jesus mentions in John 4:24, "... the hour is coming, and is now when the true worshipers will worship the Father in spirit and truth; for the Father is seeking such to worship Him. God *is* Spirit, and those who worship Him must worship in spirit and truth."

Worship ties us to our true identity because it is in our nature to worship God. When we are not praising God, then who are we worshipping? The Lord is coming back to the sons of worshippers. True worship is not about being able to sing or having a singing voice. It is about having a heart that is prostrated toward God and gives Him praise no matter what circumstances may happen.

The Lord is worthy of our praise in song and dance, in spirit and truth. The angels sing, "Holy, Holy, Holy is the Lord Almighty all day and night."[95] Everything in creation that has life worships the Lord. Even the rocks would cry out if we didn't. God has made us to sing to the Lord with joy in our hearts, knowing we belong to Him. Worshipping the Lord comes from a place of abiding in Him or, *soaking* that I mentioned earlier. Whoever abides in Him will not abide in darkness.

> *Abide in Me, and I in you. As the branch cannot bear fruit of itself, unless it abides in the vine, neither can you, unless you abide in Me.*
>
> *I am the vine, and you are the branches. He who abides in Me, and I in him, bears much fruit; for without Me, you can do nothing.*
>
> *If anyone does not abide in Me, he is cast out as a branch and is withered; and they gather them and throw them into the fire, and they are burned.*
>
> *If you abide in Me, and My words abide in you, you will ask what you desire, and it shall be done for you.*
>
> *By this, My Father is glorified, that you bear much fruit; so you will be My disciples.*
>
> *As the Father loved Me, I also have loved you;* ***abide in My love. If you keep My commandments, you will abide in My love,*** *just as I have kept My Father's commandments and abide in His love.*
>
> John 15:4-10

---

95   Revelations 4:8

Do you have something to praise God about? Every good and perfect gift comes from Him, and we are stewards of what He has given us. When we worry, our minds allow the enemy access, resulting in double mindedness. When we praise, abide, and worship the Lord when stress is in our lives, we give no foothold to the enemy in our thoughts. God's name is Faithful. When we recite the Lord's prayer, we say, "Hallowed..." which means *holy, sacred, dedicated,* and *consecrated.* "Hallowed be Your name," is "Holy be your name."[96] God is Holy, and we ought to refer to Him as Holy. For there is nothing bad or deceitful that proceeds from Him. He is pure and free from contamination in every way.

This makes His truth have so much more substance and power to live it out accordingly for His glory. "These things I have spoken to you, that My joy may remain in you, and *that* your joy may be full."[97] Do you want your joy to be full? Praise Him even when it is difficult. Abide in Him. Worship Him. Do not entertain the thoughts that are against God's nature. He wants our hearts and minds to abide in His love, and we do this by believing who He is and aligning our thoughts and behaviors to His truth.

> *"He who has my commandments
> and keeps them, it is he who loves Me.*
>
> *And he who loves Me will be
> loved by my Father and
> I will love him and manifest
> Myself to him." - Jesus*
> John 14:21

---

96   Matthew 6:9
97   John 15:11

Attitude of Believing

*"He who believes in Me believes not in Me
but in Him who sent Me."*

John 12:44

We must believe who Jesus says He is. God humbled Himself to restore humanity to Himself through His Son Jesus Christ because He knows, in our sinful nature, we could not do it on our own.

Believing Makes Things Possible

We must believe when we read His Word that He is speaking to us. When He speaks to us, we must learn how to discern His voice. We need to ask ourselves, "Are my thoughts according to God's truth, or are they false or questionable?" Our brains do not tell us what is true. We have to tell our brains what is true since many thoughts enter our minds. If we do not choose our thoughts, they will randomly pop into our brains. They may have meaning or have not been processed. This can cause us to stay stuck in our behaviors because we have yet to put each thought into its proper "file." When we do not renew our thinking, we can detour our belief system from God's sovereignty. If we do not understand who Jesus is to God or why God sent Him, then we can think our situation or circumstances are insignificant to God and continue to walk in disobedience or unbelief because of our lack of knowledge and understanding. We must submit our minds to Christ and know who God is and then His truth will take captive (hold back) the wrong thoughts.

God has said that there is no God before or after Him and that we must believe in what He says.[98] Jesus told two blind men to believe that He could heal them before He performed their healing.[99] Jesus promised that all things are possible to those that believe.[100] When we humble ourselves and admit our unbelief, Jesus is faithful and will meet us according to our faith. We just need to admit our doubts and ask Him to help us believe who He is so we can align our thinking to His heavenly kingdom culture. Heaven and the earth already know who God, Jesus, and the Holy Spirit is. Our belief system is to bring heaven to earth and believe in the power of the gospel. We see in the Bible faith aligns with believing. When we have faith, we align our thinking to heaven where there is no sickness or disease. We train our minds to stand on that truth even though we may experience otherwise. Jesus can turn our *dead* situations and make them *alive* again, whether it is physical, spiritual, financial, or emotional. When God says *all* things, we must believe *all* things. When we doubt what God can do, then we are limiting who He is. The truth is not in us when we *reason* what God is capable of.

Don't allow other people to taint your perception of who He is. Jesus was even laughed at when he said the twelve-year-old damsel was not dead but sleeping.[101] Not everyone will believe or have the faith that will get people excited to share who God is, especially when they are dealing with bitterness, anger, hurt, or pain. It's up to us to recognize what is holding us back from believing and being entirely convinced of His love for ourselves and others?

---

98   Isaiah 43:10
99   Matthew 9:28
100   Mark 9:23
101   Mark 5:39

We are to Believe in His Promises

When we are not entirely convinced of who God is, we can allow the enemy to steal the Word in our hearts and deceive us from following the truth. For our faith to take root, we must receive His Word as truth and believe in the power of Jesus.

> *And these signs shall follow them that believe; In my name shall they cast out devils; they shall speak with new tongues; they shall take up serpents; and if they drink any deadly thing, it shall not hurt them; they shall lay hands on the sick, and they shall recover.*
> Mark 16:17-18

> *We should not be afraid of those who speak in tongues or those who are resilient to sickness and toxicity, and we should not be slow in the heart to believe.*
> Luke 24:25

Even Jesus asked, "How can we believe in His words if we do not believe in His writings?"[102] The Holy Spirit helps us with His truth. He teaches us and leads us to know our Father.

Many promises come with believing. When we confess Jesus before men, Jesus will confess us before the Father. The only way to get to the Father is through Jesus, so it is part of our faith to share who He is and what He has done for us.

---

102   John 5:47

"If you believe you will see the glory of God
If you believe in Him, you shall not die but live.
If you believe you live in the light,
you will become the sons and daughters of the light."

"Fruit bears the closest relation to light.
The sun pours a continuous flood of light
into the fruits, and they furnish
the best portion of food a human being
requires for the sustenance
of mind and body." [103]
–Amos Bronson Alcott

The Bible refer to bearing good fruit in our lives many times. When we die to ourselves, we are fulfilling God's Word and walking according to the spirit rather than the flesh.

Not only so, but we, who have the firstfruits of the Spirit, groan inwardly as we wait eagerly for our adoption to sonship, the redemption of our bodies. For in this hope we were saved. But hope that is seen is no hope at all. Who hopes for what they already have? But if we hope for what we do not yet have, we wait for it patiently. In the same way, the Spirit helps us in our weakness. We do not know what we ought to pray for, but the Spirit himself intercedes for us through wordless groans. He who searches our hearts knows the mind of the Spirit because the Spirit intercedes for God's people in accordance with the will of God.
Romans 8:23-27

We have the capacity to grow in the Spirit in His likeness.

---

103   Alcott, 46

Our Words are Seeds We Plant Daily

For even when God spoke, light came to be. We can see that God's spoken Word created the separation of waters, plant life, the sun, the moon, and the stars. We see the sea was filled with living creatures and animals were brought forth from the earth. God created and upheld all things by the Word of His power.

From our words, we produce the fountain of life, as it is written, "... the lips of the righteous feed many..."[104] Also, "The tongue of the wise bring healing,"[105] and "...the mouth of the upright delivers men..."[106] To do the will of our Father, we must believe that He sent Jesus as our Mediator (to reconcile us to God), Intercessor (to intercede on our behalf to God), and Judge (to judge our work according to His righteous standards).

> *Then said they unto him, 'What shall we do, that we might work the works of God?' Jesus answered and said unto them: 'this is the work of God, that you believe in Him whom He has sent.'*
> John 6:29

> *And the Word was made flesh, and dwelt among us, (and we beheld His glory, the glory of the only begotten of the Father,) full of grace and truth.*
> John 1:14

When we believe in Jesus, we behold His glory. Jesus was in the

---

104   Proverbs 10:21
105   Proverbs 12:18
106   Proverbs 12:6

bosom of His Father, knowing Him intimately. Jesus gives us the mystery of who God is when we build a relationship with Him.

Attitude of Giving

Giving Back to the Lord *Increases Our Faith*

Giving back to the Lord displays in *whom* we trust. Do you trust in yourself or money or do you trust in God who gives you the resources? When we give, we cannot guarantee that what we give will be used for the greater good of God's purposes. I have heard many times that people do not want to give to a church because they believe it only goes to their building. I think some churches may have taken advantage of their members by not being honest about where the money goes. If that is important to you, you may need to find another church that is honest with their spending and where you feel comfortable to give. I love how our church, The Crossing, provides a report at the end of every year showing what they spent, donated, tithed, and kept for their church. We know clearly where our money is going, and we know ultimately that our money belongs to the Lord. Where my church decides to put that money is good with me, as long as it is doing *His* kingdom work.

God Wants Us to be Cheerful Givers

If we give grudgingly, then why give? God knows our hearts on whether we want to give. I think it's that simple. If you don't see the blessing or purpose of giving back to the Lord, then what is the point in doing it? This is the only area in which I see God asks us to test Him.[107] I believe God works faithfully *for* us when we give. He gives us benefits that we may not understand or comprehend just on this principle of tithing, alone. It is putting our trust into someone we cannot see and then trusting His provision for our lives. When I started tithing, I gave what I *could*, first taking care of what I needed for my bills, home, and personal life and then gave the rest. I looked for opportunities to give to people who needed it. I was able to bless people and give back more because I had learned how to be content in all seasons. I learned when I had more money than what I needed for myself, I was able to bless others more abundantly.

Faith Resembles a Mustard Seed

A small seed can grow into a glorious tree with many branches. This is like faith in our lives growing into fullness because of the things we hope for. When we give, we have hope that it will bless others, and that they will spend it on what they need, but we do not control their actions. To remain faithful to God, we must think that no matter what we give, we believe we are giving it to the Lord. We can easily have our hope in God yet live as though everything belongs to us. We tend to talk ourselves out of blessing others because we do not know what they will do with the resource or money. Everything belongs to the Lord. We must even be mindful of who is coming after us and what legacy we will leave behind so others can thrive. We arrived naked, and we'll go home naked. It is good to save money and leave an inheritance for our children, but the Bible doesn't stop there, it states, "He who is wise, leaves an inheritance for his children's children."[108] Many of us are not wise. My family has not left this inheritance, and it is rare to hear

107   Malachi 3:10
108   Proverbs 13:22

of anyone doing this. If we want to make a difference for our families, we need to think about what we will leave behind. So often, we spend check by check, not doing anything but spending money on food and greedy desires.

> But they that will be rich fall into temptation and a snare, and **into** many **foolish and hurtful lusts**, which drown men in destruction and perdition. For the love of money is the root of all evil: which while some coveted after, they have erred from the faith, and pierced themselves through with many sorrows.
> 1 Timothy 6:9-10

Spending our money on excess food and clothes can set us up for temptation. We can err from our faith due to our spending and coveting. Ask yourself, "Do I need what I am thinking about buying?" Or "Who can I help today?" I wonder what would happen if we honored God with His money? If we learned how to be content with what we have, would we give to those in need, cheerfully? Would things change in our society? I think so. Caring for one another more than ourselves and lending more, can become a powerful statement that communicates to an unbeliever. It might prompt them to think, "I want to do what they are doing because it demonstrates love and unity." Remember we are to draw people into our lives, by looking *attractive*, and we do this by doing things that the world has not seen or heard.

Our faith can grow by trusting God to take care of our needs concerning what we wear and eat. For He promises to be faithful when we apply our anxieties to Him in prayer and petition, with thanksgiving by making our requests known (Philippians 4:6). We learn to not put confidence in what we can do, put in who God is. We learn to trust that He takes care of us, for He knows the laying down and getting up of man (Psalm 139:2) and considers us more than sparrows (Matthew 10:31).

Everyone is looking for a place to belong. Giving makes others feel important, and it shows we care. We do it as part of our nature because it is who we are in Christ. Since God has demonstrated His love (gift) for us through Jesus, we can show it to others. He even tells us to try Him or test Him in the area of tithing:

> *"Bring all the tithes into the storehouse, That there may be food in My house, And **try Me** now in this, "Says the LORD of hosts." If I will not open for you the windows of heaven And pour out for you such blessing, That **there will not be room enough to receive it."***
> Malachi 3:10

We can decree God's Word back to Him and tell Him, "You have made a promise to us when we tithe, so Father, we will thank You for our blessing that pours over to others in our space and influence." I cannot wait for the windows of heaven to open and for the outpouring of the blessing to be received!

> *"But a generous man devises generous things, and **by generosity, he shall stand."***
> Isaiah 32:8

Be Kingdom-Minded

In Jesus, we have boldness and access to the Father with confidence through faith in Jesus.[109] Through the Holy Spirit, we can know what our Father is doing. As children of God, we have power, love, and a sound mind. He gives us the boldness as His children the more we grow in our relationship with Jesus. *Access* means *entering into a room* or *a means of approaching.* This means we can go to Jesus with confidence like coming into a room where He wants to hear from us. We can boldly make our requests known to Him because He desires us to come to Him in faith, expecting that He will meet the desires of our hearts. God has a throne room where He invites us to enter.

Imagine God's throne room is a Holy place where God receives all our requests. When we enter, we do it with thankfulness that He hears us, we praise Him with reverence and expectancy, and we ask Him for the things concerning our loved ones and us. Some of us are at different places in our prayer life and believe everything He has promised us is ours and belongs to us in Christ Jesus. Confessing Jesus as Lord in our lives gives us boldness to pray with a decree and declaration that our time is "right on time" for where God has us. Some of us are still not quite sure if God will meet all our needs, so we question the fact that He cares or hears us. But faith is not doubting who Jesus is and what He has done for us.

Faith is testifying what He has done so we remember that even though we may not see our prayers answered right away, He is faithful and just and we are not to give up asking and believing that He can and will meet our expectations. We are members of

109   Ephesians 3:10

the household of God; we **belong to a royal kingdom**. This world is not our home; we should always be thinking more of who God is, so we do not have our hearts set in this world. This world and people will disappoint us, but God won't disappoint us, for He loves us with an everlasting love. This is the case, even though we may not understand it at times because of the suffering we face. With suffering comes humility because we confess we need a Savior and know that we cannot do this life on our own. We must rely on and trust in our God, but we cannot do this without knowing who we are.

In the Bible, Hannah knew her identity
as a maidservant unto the Lord.
As she was waiting on the Lord,
she knew her position as a servant.
Hannah did not receive a child from the Lord
until she hit "rock bottom."
She was so grieved in her spirit
by not being able to have children
that she cried out to the Lord
and told Him she would devote her child
back to Him. God blessed her with a child,
but not just for her. It was for His will
to raise up the last judge for Israel.

God Searches for Hearts that Give Back to Him

Sometimes our pain and suffering lead us to cry out because we become grieved. Those are the exact moments we can pour out our wants and needs which allows us to act accordingly to God's plan for His people. Many of us forget that we are servants of the Lord. Even Paul considered himself a bond servant. Yet, in today's culture, we may think, "I'm highly favored. God will give me what I want and bless what I touch." We may not allow Him to guide and lead us, but rather live from our selfish desires. Just because we are servants doesn't mean we don't have favor.

Elkanah gave a worthy portion to Hannah, his wife, because he loved her. When your spouse married you, it was because he or she loved you. If you're not married, God is your husband, and He loves you. No matter if we are married or not, we are favored by our Heavenly Father. He says we are fearfully and wonderfully made.[110] We have the same attributes as God, because we are made in His image, full of His glory. Because we carry His glory, He will shine His favor in our lives because of the inheritance we receive when we become His.

We do not know to which measure the Holy Spirit will give to us; God gives to the Holy Spirit without measure. We cannot assume we know if someone has God's favor since it rains on the just and the unjust.[111] Therefore, we are not called to judge someone but to love them because that is the heart of our Father. When we have mastered His truth above our feelings, we are able to be perfect as He is perfect.

The Promises of God

There are promises of God inside us, and God does not want us to be distracted by people, places, or things or by the things going on

110 Psalm 139:14
111 Matthew 5:45

around us through offense, arguments, and sins. Remember, the kingdom of God is inside us. We hold the keys to our future, but if we never get over the past or stay in contention, how can we press into what He has for us?

There are different times and seasons for each of us, and those that precede us strengthen and encourage us, just as the next generation coming up. Those in a season of reaping what they have sown encourage the planters and harvesters. We are to help build one another up and bring unity in the church. When non-Christians see what we are doing, it may inspire them to want to know what we have that makes us different. We are to be attractive to the world and set apart for His glory. We can't do that if we're comparing ourselves, have self-hatred, envy, or jealousy in any way.

Let's Honor One Another More than Ourselves

We honor others by meeting people where they are in their journey of faith and supporting them to live a life worthy of the calling He has given as stewards of His word. A self-sacrificial love (*agape*) can be learned in our marriages. When we are single, we do things on "our" terms, but when we are married, we learn to give in this area. This is a sacrifice, but it shouldn't stop there; sacrifice and love can grow with all our relationships.

We must be able to identify what we might be avoiding when choosing not to love? Could it be self-hatred, fear, or insecurity? What must we do to overcome this behavior? When we do not choose to honor others, we are putting our ego and pride above God (who sees us all through His Son, Jesus). He sees us as righteous because of what Jesus did on the cross. His blood sanctifies us, makes us whole and clean. Our behaviors should not define who we are, but rather we should be defined by to whom we belong, as children of God. Honoring others implies others are just as important as we are to God.

Let the love of Christ dwell deep inside of you and hold Him in such high esteem that it makes people curious to know your God. He gives us blessings not because we are good but because He is righteous. We honor and bless others because He has been good to us. We reveal who He is when we respond in love towards others because of how He sees them, rather than reacting out of fear, doubt, or insecurity.

Attitude of a Child

We have a Father in heaven who will meet all our needs. No one is like Him or comparable to Him. He is our personal God, and is loving, caring, selfless, giving, guiding, teaching, patient, long-suffering, kind, and so much more. He is living inside of us when we accept His Son Jesus Christ as our Lord and Savior. He knows our thoughts, feelings, fears, and joys. Nothing is a surprise to Him, but it does not mean we do not grieve our Father. He has feelings too.

He knows how many and what kind of blessings to give. He knows what we can handle and what not to provide us with. He knows how to withhold from us. He knows our laying down and waking up. He watches us, sings over us, and dances with us. He cherishes us as His beautiful handiwork. He created us good and is delighted to do life with us. Children are usually not afraid to ask their parents for what they want. They may pressure their parents and badger them, repeatedly asking, but having no idea why their parents might yell and tell them to stop asking. Our Heavenly Father will not yell at us when we ask Him for what we want. Instead, He invites us to keep on asking, to seek Him and not give up.

Luke 18 tells of a widow that constantly knocked on the door of a judge, saying, "Avenge me of my adversary."[112] For some time he refused, but because she was persistent, he finally gave her what she wanted. Now picture Jesus being our Judge. He goes to the Father for us. We must know that even though this judge in the story did not fear God or care what people think, we know God, who is our faithful Judge and Father, will give to us so much more because we are His children.

God wants to give good gifts to us because we are His children.[113] We have not, because we ask not, and we may not ask because we do not see ourselves as *worthy* of asking. We still sing songs that call us a "wretched" and "sinners," yet God sees us as "saints" and "heirs." When Paul referred to the new believers, he called them saints.[114] You are a saint. Being a saint is not determined by what you have done, instead, it has been established on who God is and what He has done for us through His Son, Jesus. Being a saint is part of your inheritance when you have accepted Jesus as your Lord and Savior.

When we change our mindsets to see ourselves through His lens, we will understand how He made us worthy. Our friend Jesus laid

112   Luke 18:3
113   Luke 11:13
114   Romans 1:7

his life down for us, and there is no greater love than the gesture He did for us. Since we believe in all of who He is, we also receive His inheritance as a citizen of heaven. What our Father has belongs to us, which gives us permission to ask. When we ask, we do not ask out of selfish ambition, but we ask in alignment with His heart. Parents want to give their children the desires of their hearts and instinctively know if something is bad or wrong for them. When parents agree with what their children ask for, hearts are aligned. It is purposeful, just as God has a purpose for us.

Have an Attitude of Curiosity

Children are curious. They may ask questions over and over until they get the answer that satisfies them. What has happened to our curiosity as adults? Do we think we know it all? Is there anything else for us to know? When we look to our Father to know what He thinks of us and fill ourselves with His words, we will live out the confidence that can only be found in Him. We will be bold and live courageously because we are spending time with Him. When we spend time with our Creator, He reflects His light on us, and we become His reflection. It's like driving with our high beams on in darkness. We will know our next step because He is the one highlighting and showing us the way to go.

Attitude of Remembrance

You may not have been told this before, but you are a forgetter. You cannot remember everything. That is why we take notes. Many of us learn in many ways. Some of us are visual learners, some of us are hearers, some of us like to read, but no matter the difference, we are all learners. We did not come into life to do absolutely nothing; we all came into this world for a purpose. Some find it sooner than others, and some die without knowing their purpose. When I was living a life full of myself, I did not think about *my purpose*. I just thought, "Live life to the fullest, 'till I die." That is pathetic now as I look back at it. If we don't know the Lord, we do not know ourselves. If that is the case, how can anyone possibly know their purpose? Some people are born talented with extreme skills. However, their talent could easily be used for the wrong reason. This doesn't mean that God can't restore it, but to truly live out what God has for us, we must remember what He has brought us through. This way we are able to live beyond those detours in life and not make those same mistakes again. We can learn the new path that He gives us. The Lord asks us to remember the things He has done and instructs us to tell our children, so we do not forget. This will teach our children who He is. I wonder just how important this is?

Remember the Lord made everything,
and the earth and heavens belong to Him.
Remember to keep your focus on Him,
not on your problems or circumstances.
Remember His promises.
Remember what He has done.
Remember what He will do.
Remember who you are in Him.
Remember what you do today,
will be for your future generations to come.

Imagine a generation not remembering what the Lord has done. What do you think would happen? Do you think the following generations would still know God and His wonderful works? Maybe, but over time, it will fade, and they may not remember anything. If no one is doing God's Word or talking about it, how will the people remember or know who their God is?

Between the last book in the Old Testament
and the New Testament,
there are 400 years in which God was silent.
Before then, God spoke to the
people all the time,
even through His prophets and angels.
It sounds like the people did not
remember the Lord
their God when God became silent.
Think about God being silent in your life.
Would you do what you want to do or would
you still follow Him and live by faith?

Think about Noah and the ark. God only decided to save His family because Noah was the only one who remembered the Lord. Noah was righteous in God's eyes. In the days to come, the Lord remembered him and his family and saved them from the flood. The Lord gave them a new beginning.

How many of us *wish* we had a new beginning?
We wish others didn't look at us by our past behavior.
We wish our past circumstances didn't define us.
We wish people could move on from the past
and forget the things we have done,
but unfortunately, people may want to keep us
where they last remembered us.
Then the real question becomes:
how do we move forward in this new beginning
after accepting Jesus Christ as our Lord and Savior?

Where Christ's blood has washed us *clean,*
and there is no condemnation
for those in Christ Jesus.
Where we prepare ourselves
for Christ's return for a church
that has no spot or blemish,
living life in faith no matter what
others may think or say.

Our lives are now hidden with Christ in God. *Hidden* implies both *concealment* and *safety*, both *invisibility* and *security*. Christ said He was going where "...the world will not see Me anymore..."[115] Paul added a new focus of the believers' attention. He taught they should look upward to Christ's reign over them in heaven and forward to His return for them in the clouds.

---

115   John 14:19

Running the Race

We are to run our race since we are surrounded by a great cloud of witnesses. Paul instructs us to:

> *"...lay aside every weight, and the sin which so easily ensnares us, and let us run with endurance the race that is set before us, looking unto Jesus, the author, and finisher of our faith, who for the joy that was set before Him endured the cross, despising the shame, and has sat down at the right hand of the throne of God."*
> Hebrews 12:1-2
>
> *Those who run in a race all run, but only one receives the prize. Run in such a way that you may obtain it.*
>
> *Know that everyone who competes for the prize is temperate in all things, and they do it to obtain a perishable crown, but we for an imperishable crown.*
>
> *Therefore do not run with uncertainty. But fight: not as one who beats the air (as though it is for nothing).*
>
> *But discipline your body (mind, thoughts, and behavior) and bring it into subjection (under Christ), so when you have shared with others, you shall not become disqualified.*
> 1 Corinthians 9:24-27

Prepare your mind for action, strengthen your heart through patience, pray in supplication, and *run the race before you.*

CHAPTER TWO
BODY

YOUR **BODY** IS HIS TEMPLE

"I discipline my body like an athlete,
training it to do what it should.
Otherwise, I fear that after preaching to others,
I myself might be disqualified."

1 Corinthians 9:27 [NLT]

Be Diligent

Diligence is man's precious possession.[116] In a race, all the runners run, but only one receives the prize. Nowadays, it seems like we get a trophy *just* for participating, where it appears to discourage motivation to win the prize, since everyone wins. We quit when things get difficult or when we feel like we'd rather be doing something else. But if we think about the ability to win a prize, we have to recognize it doesn't come without a process.

In order to run, we first have to walk, by taking a step, one foot in front of the other. We are unable to do this well without learning how to stand and keep our balance. Our foundation *or body* may be unstable. We may have forgotten this process because we were so young when we first learned how to walk, but if we pay attention to infants, we will recognize that we *all* started the same way, by learning. Many people may equate falling with failing, but what if we looked at falling as learning? When we are learning something

---

116   Proverbs 12:27

new, we aren't going to be as good as we hoped, so, we have to fall a few times before we can fully apply the new skill. When we learn to trust ourselves with the process, we will turn our crawling into walking, our walking into running, and then experience what our feet, balance, and mobility can do.

Some of us will even take risks without knowing what to expect, being unafraid to *try*. We learn how to run short and long distances and find a way to adapt our breathing to maintain the right stamina. We adjust our bodies to endure hills and valleys. If we look at what an athlete does, we see they cannot overindulge in food or eat the bare minimum. They learn their portions and find out what is best for their bodies. An athlete doesn't allow his mind to think negatively. He tells himself, "I'm going to win this," not out of arrogance but out of the belief of putting in his best work and doing his optimal to achieve greatness. An athlete doesn't decide to sleep in because he doesn't feel like training; he gets up and goes anyway. He will fight through negative thoughts and challenges that stand in his way. He will have a focused determination to win or succeed in his goal and make arrangements to sacrifice other things for what he wants. He prepares for hard work, becomes dedicated to his vision, and will go for it despite life's distractions and circumstances. He doesn't look at the disadvantages but focuses on the possibilities and perseveres no matter what.

For our faith to grow, we must be able to move, *physically*. God says we will run and not grow weary. We are required to proceed. We are mandated to move. Yet sometimes we don't. We would rather sit in front of the television, iPad or computer, and pray for results but not put anything into action. When we discipline our bodies to get up in the morning for work, it's because we have to. We want that job and security to get paid. If we don't care about our job or the money, we won't get up. There would be no purpose in going to work, but if we have a reason to go, we find it in ourselves to get up and *go*.

For many of us, working out is a choice. I used to think it was a choice for me, but the older I get, the more I see it is beneficial for me. I work out because it makes me feel better, look better, stay focused, feel young again, and most importantly, I'm taking care of God's temple. The problem is, I love to eat, so when I don't work out, I can see the pounds instantly on my body. It's not a good look for me, and neither is it a good feeling. There would be moments that I would wait to feel like working out, but that would never come. I never felt motivated to work out even after the feasts of the holidays. I would think about working out, then be mad at myself for not doing it. Being mad at myself never *made* me *want to* go work out. Instead, it would cause me to remain in my guilt and shame, and stay where I was, *doing* nothing.

Subject Our Bodies to be Disciplined

Being disciplined is not easy, in fact, many of us have strived to live an easy-going life, trying not to do anything that requires effort and quitting when things became difficult. To be disciplined is a rarity nowadays, but that is what God calls us to do. To submit our thoughts to be under Christ's, we must teach our minds to know what is right from wrong in His eyes, and then we can put it into practice. Disciplining our bodies may include getting up every morning, spending time with God in His Word, and creating daily habits even though we may feel like sleeping in and don't feel like reading. We can choose to discipline ourselves to put in the work even when we want to relax, scroll on Facebook, or watch TV. Perhaps if we tried thinking of discipline as an act of passion, we might get to see how spending time with a loving Father who created us no longer seems like a "chore" or "discipline." Rather, we can be excited to be with someone who makes us feel loved and valued. God *has called us to spend time with Him*. Even when He called the disciples to follow Him, they were with Him for some time before they were able to perform miracles. If we reason and compare ourselves to what others are doing, we might be steered away from what God has *called* us to do.

Reasoning is Behind Our Lack of Motivation

Through reasoning we see things from our perspective, and we don't necessarily make wise decisions. I have heard and seen many testimonies where God has helped women with their weight and eating habits. Yet, as much as I have cried out to Him (without action), I didn't see Him helping me. Is it because of my lack of self-discipline or lack of self-control? Perhaps I need to put faith in my actions besides just asking for help? I negatively began to think, "God cares about other people more than me. He is willing to help others, more than me. I'm not important to Him." *These are lies.* I'm not sure why God hasn't helped me in this circumstance, but it doesn't mean He loves me any less.

When we think these thoughts, we may think the unbiblical statement, "God only helps those who help themselves." This quote can come off as though God doesn't care about us, or that we have to do something for God to hear us. Although faith is an action and He CAN help me without me doing anything about it, it is His decision.

I act out in faith when I choose to believe He is good no matter how I feel about myself.

I'm walking in faith when I choose to do something about my eating, (like fasting or changing my diet), or doing something physical (like working out or going for a walk). When I turn from my normal behavior of comfort and instead do something that makes me feel uncomfortable, (like going to the gym), I quote scriptures in my head and declare His Word over myself.

Having my thoughts focused on Him gives me faith that He will make the time go faster and help me through it. Having Him in my mind always helps me workout harder. I declare it's His strength that gets me through, because I know I'd rather be doing something else or nothing at all. Self-talk is vital to having a healthy relationship with God, yourself, and others. Remember our God is personal, and He wants you to invite Him intimately into your life, for the big and the small things.

Faith Takes Time and Perseverance

We may not see automatic results right away, and if we do, there may be a season where it doesn't seem easy. Remaining faithful in our discipline and obedience when we do not see results, is the testing of our faith. To persevere, we will go through trials, hardships, and misunderstandings. To overcome this, we must put our faith into action! It's not that God did not help me with my body; it's *the way I perceived it*. I will not understand His work always within my life, but I must understand His truth leads and guides me and is still with me, even when I *feel* as though it isn't. His word is truth, and we must look to it as a basis of our faith.

Our speech should show we are Christians. God is clear that what comes out of our mouths, defiles us, and this includes our language. He commissions us to put off anger, wrath, malice, blasphemy, lying, and filthy language.[117] We can quickly become frustrated to the point that we may curse God, ourselves, and those we love, but this will cause more damage than good. I believe the way we speak matters in any given situation, especially to ourselves.

As a little girl, I was not taught
about positive affirmations,
in fact, I didn't think there was a purpose
to me living at all.
Nobody said *I mattered*.
Then, I found a book that talked
about me being 'worth' it.
I found out that there must be a purpose
to why I am here.
Even though the book talked about a 'divine,'
I knew it was God.
I knew I needed to say prayers
that would incorporate
Him into my life and I needed to start
seeing myself how God sees me because,
in my mind, I had so much doubt and confusion.
God cares about how I treat my body,
and even what I say about myself.
Every time I put myself down,

---

117   Colossians 3:8

or think that I'm not good enough,
complain or judge myself,
I'm doing this not just to myself,
but ultimately to the Lord.
I'm complaining against God.
I'm telling Him, "What you made isn't good enough."
I'm sure this doesn't make Him pleased with me.
For it is contrary to His Word.
For me to get out of this 'stinkin' thinkin',
I have to remember that I belong to Him,
He made me perfect, whole
and complete and since He made me,
I ought to trust that I am precious in His sight.

"Whether we live or die we belong to the Lord."
Romans 14:8

Belonging to the Lord means we are not our own, but belong to God, since we were bought with a price. His Son Jesus died on the cross for our *sins, transgressions, and iniquities.* Thinking about His truth doesn't make it easy for me to stop condemning myself. Instead, it's a good start to love and accept who I am, where I am, and stop thinking I need to be *perfect* before anyone else can love me. Perfection leaves no room for improvement and since I am always learning how to improve to be like His Son, I can accept that God will not be done with me until I go home to be with Him.

Loving ourselves takes time and patience. It's understanding that we don't need to condemn ourselves (for there is no condemnation for those in Christ Jesus), but we still might, especially when we are alone. Condemning is also complaining and blaming. Making a statement about being fat, stupid, or ignorant, is complaining. Making a statement about how things are our fault, creates the mindset that God has flaws and has lied to us in some way. Stating a fact about infirmity and accepting it, says we believe what we *see* but, having faith in Jesus is the *substance* we cannot see, the things we hope for in Christ Jesus. We can see ourselves being whole, a friend, and complete. To love ourselves is to remind ourselves that what God made is good. You, my friend, are beautiful and cherished by our Creator.

Faith is the Substance

"Now faith is the substance
of things hoped for,
the evidence of things not seen."
Hebrews 1:11

We can choose to believe what has already been accomplished on the cross. Just because someone may tell you a fact, doesn't mean it is necessarily true. As believers, we hold our truth on our God, Jesus Christ. We constantly must speak who we are in Him. There is no sickness or disease (dis-ease) in heaven. We actively must speak out that we are healed even though we may not believe it in our hearts. Even, if we do not believe yet, when we say it, our feelings can catch up with our thoughts and then ultimately that belief can sink into our hearts. It just takes time and persistence. When we speak out loud and hear our own words, something is activated in our brains and these words penetrate, as our inner truth.

Just think about how much negativity you talk about yourself and others. It may take a plethora of positive statements to believe that you are healed or believe that *you* matter to change things. Confessing that Jesus Christ is our Lord is the same way God wants us to confess our healing, confess our sins to one another, and confess our testimonies. It begins with the words we speak. When God decided to make creation, He did it with His voice. He spoke and there it was. God said, "Let there be light," and it happened.[118] When God decided to create us in His image, it was in His likeness that He made us. He even made us in His likeness to create. We get to create with our minds, words, thoughts, and bodies. Our very being is creative. Yet, we haven't been able to understand who God made us be.

We think that if we do this or that, then *that* must be who we are, but who we are is not in what we do. What we do stems from how God made us. It is our purpose and our value. However, if we do not know who we are (children of God), then we can easily misuse our creativity for the enemy. We can easily talk ourselves out of our greatness because we do not feel like we have the potential to accomplish great things, but greatness lives in us. It is the Holy Spirit. "Greater is He that is in you than in the world." [119]

He Who Guards His Mouth Preserves His Life

"Out of the same mouth come praise and cursing. My brothers and sisters, this should not be."[120] (James 3:10). Slander, filthy language, or abrasive speech is shameful and should not be used by His

118   Genesis 1:3
119   1 John 4:4
120   James 3:10

servants. We cannot get to where we want to go without declaring it with our words and speaking as if it were already true. It is by faith we proclaim Jesus is Lord, so it is by faith we profess we are healed, saved, and delivered. Does it mean that the facts don't exist? No, but what it does mean is that we are deciding that regardless of what we see, we are choosing to believe in what Jesus has already given us on the cross. He knows the end from the beginning, and even though the facts may say we have an ailment, we believe that in the Spirit we are healed and seated with Jesus in heaven. Since there is no sickness in heaven, then it must mean that we are healed! Pleasant words are like a honeycomb, sweetness to the soul, and health to the bones.[121] What goes on inside of our souls, is manifested in our bodies.

Pleasant Words are Sweetness to the Soul

What we hear or say to others, matters to our souls. Pleasant words produce life that is more beautiful than if we were to speak harsh words to each other. What we fill our souls with is revealed through the body and can either bring health or sickness. Those who say, "I'm going to get sick," usually end up sick because they keep talking about it. They are saying words that produce sickness. When we are self-critical about how we look, we will continue to stay there because we are cursing (speaking against) the way God made us. When we judge others or gossip, we are causing division amongst ourselves, which will keep us apart. God does not want division between us, but until we start speaking life (sweetness) over ourselves, we will not be able to love others accordingly.

---

121   Proverbs 16:24

When God said, "Let there be light," He did not waver in what He said. He spoke it, and it was. We have that same power, yet we take it lightly and are not aware of the power of our words. "Truth" is for the followers of the one who is the "Truth."[122] Since we walk by faith and not by sight, we know that "truth" is what God sees as truth. It goes beyond our feelings and comprehension when we speak His truth, (rather than speaking what we see or feel). The phrase, "...on earth, as it is in heaven..." means speaking His truth that exists in heaven, where there is no sickness or disease, along with the victory already being won in Christ Jesus.

I love the book, *The Hidden Messages in Water,* by Masaru Emoto. Dr. Emoto believed the physical structure of water could be changed by our emotional "energies" and "vibrations" and that water was a "blueprint for our reality." He discovered, "...water serves as a transporter of energy throughout our bodies. The transport of energy is similar to a car that moves throughout the body. If the body is clogged and soiled, then the cargo in the car will also become filthy, and so it is essential that the water remains clean."[123]

Our bodies are made up of roughly 70 percent water, which is said to depreciate as we get older. Because we are made of water, it is important to find how it interacts with nature. For water to "remain clean," we have to say and think kind things to ourselves, because water can be changed by our emotional "energies." The thoughts in our minds will show in our bodies. That is how powerful our thoughts are! So, imagine how much more powerful your words are!

---

122   John 14:6
123   Emoto, M. pg. xvii

Vibration is Powerful

We can change our emotions and attitude by what we think and say to ourselves and even humming and singing to ourselves can produce cleanliness to our bodies.

> One day, I watched a television show
> on how a young girl was called a "snail caller."
> She did it by humming to the snail
> so the snail would come out of its shell.
> It was amazing to think that a humming sound,
> not words, would get these snails to show themselves.
> We can consider this as proof that by vibration,
> our emotional status can change
> and make us want to come out of our shell (or self).

You can transport clean water through your body by stating kind and generous words, not just to yourself, but to others. Even in hardships, we cannot wait for our circumstances to change before we decide to praise God. The Apostle Paul in the Bible instructs us to "...speak to one another with psalms, hymns, and songs from the Spirit. Sing and make music from your heart to the Lord."[124] When we shift our perspective to focus and praise God, no matter the situation, our true self will eventually come out of its shell.

What do I mean about our true self? God has created us more powerful than we may realize, and life has come against us with its disappointments and polluted ways. We generate the momentum to

---

124   Ephesians 5:19

go where we want to go with our sound. When we choose to change
our perspectives and shift our attitudes, that is our true selves,
letting go of all hindrances and being who God made us, as powerful.

Think about how much more we need to encourage ourselves when
we hear or experience bad news. Being in Las Vegas during the
mass shooting, many people were questioning, "What is happening
to this world"? We cannot assume that bad things do not happen to
good people; it seems as though bad things happen to all kinds of
people. It doesn't matter to whom it happens. As much as events
bring confusion to people, there is a promise that the darkness will
not overcome the light, which was shown in Las Vegas.

Many organizations and churches gather to hold prayer vigils and
worship concerts. They provided free uber rides and resources and
helped deliver food and water to hospitals and the police force. Two
policemen died on duty that night while trying to protect people.
We must remember, as a human, we have a soul that will have a
destination when we are done with this life. When it's our time to go,
we have to believe God is the master of our souls. God does not want
us to be afraid of the one who can kill the body and not the soul, but
rather to fear Him, who can destroy both soul and body in hell.[125]

Las Vegas is full of light and darkness, but the darkness will not
overcome us. I love my city and believe God is doing amazing things
here. Some may only see it for 'one thing,' but God sees it as a city
that belongs to Him. Where sin abounds, grace abounds more.[126] We
have an opportunity to be the light in dark places and to show others

---

125   Matthew 10:28
126   Romans 5:20

how to get to the Light.

Finding commonality with people allows others to soften their hearts and receive what you may be trying to say in forms of hope or faith. It comes by being their servant in areas that they may be weak (such as praying when they do not have faith or hope for their situation). It's coming alongside them in their anguish and disbelief and finding one hopeful thing in their life. It's bringing faith into a situation rather than keeping it out. We can redirect hope by proclaiming a positive outcome amid weariness. Sometimes just sitting with people not saying anything but singing a hymn or humming something praiseworthy is sufficient when bad things happen to us and those around us.

We can build our faith when we piggyback off someone else's. We need to reach out and ask for prayer from someone who has faith in something we don't. Their faith will give us enlightenment and joy to know how to pray more courageously. We feed off one another. We mimic each other. That's normal and is what we should be doing because it brings people closer to the Lord.

Imagine Our Prayer Life Changing

Our prayer life can grow by changing from asking Him for something He has already done, to thanking Jesus that we are seated with Him. That is a big difference. Our prayers should line up with the way Jesus prayed. Since we are heirs with Jesus, we must know that God is not just His Father, but ours as well. We pray to our Father. Jesus is God, but we do not pray to Him, for we know, Jesus prays for us to our Father, even today. However, everything is done through

Jesus; that is why we ask in His name. Prayer is our worship and devotion to God. It is saying we know we can't do this without Him. It is releasing what He can do on earth. Imagine the impossible and pray like God can and will do it, no matter what others may think or say. When prayers are answered we see how much He loves us. It builds our relationship with Jesus. The timing may not always be when we expect it but persevering and patience is what He teaches us when our prayers are not answered right away.

Constantly Grow in the Spirit

To grow in the Spirit means desiring the things of God. As we mature in Christ, we should keep in mind to hate the things He hates and love the things He loves. This will ensure that we are going in His direction and keeping the mind of God. Galatians is an excellent source to go to.

> But the fruit of the Spirit is love, joy, peace, longsuffering, gentleness, goodness, faith, meekness, temperance: against such, there is no law. And they that are Christ's have crucified the flesh with the affections and lusts. If we live in the Spirit, let us also walk in the Spirit. Let us not be desirous of vain glory, provoking one another, envying one another.
> Galatians 5:22-26

We have the capacity to run from the things that tempt us and to choose something else (make wise, godly decisions), rather than doing what is comfortable out of habit. We are the ones who can stand in the gap for our bloodlines and make a difference for the coming generations. It takes work to put it into practice.

I love the book of Nehemiah because
he prayed to the Lord,
it was right after he found out that
the Jerusalem wall had been torn down.
In his prayer, he reminded God of who He is:
Great, Magnificent, Merciful and Faithful.
He remembered what the Lord promised
to those who did and did not keep
His commandments, asking humbly
for the Lord to hear his prayer.

Nehemiah confessed the sins of the children of Israel
and included himself and his father's house
who has sinned and then reminded God
what would happen to the children
if they returned to Him. He confessed
that he was a servant who desired
to fear His name and requested
to prosper as His servant
and be granted mercy to rebuild the wall.
Nehemiah did something about
what he saw needed to be done.

Many times, we pray for God to take things away from us or to rebuild our lives around us, but we never initiate the change in us, for God to do something through us. When we become desperate enough, we change. We're able to get to a place of recognizing that God has a purpose for us and purposed something in our hearts to live out, that the rest of the body of Christ needs. Others may not realize what God has intended for us, and they may even laugh when we start, but what God has called us to do, He will stir inside us until we act it out. As Nehemiah built the wall, many thought it wouldn't last, and many were laughing at the vision, but when he showed the people his vision and talked about God being with Him in this project, they got on board. When they saw others joining, they too got involved. It became contagious. When their enemies saw that it was working out for them, they became frightened and plotted to come against them. God intervened, and the Israelites knew their plan and decided to gear up and put on their armor while rebuilding the wall.[127]

They Became Watchful

In society, we tend to 'people watch' at the parks or in public places or we watch television, but we may fail to watch the way Jesus calls us to. *Watch* occurs 61 times in the King James Version, which tells us, we too, must become watchful. Think about Jesus telling his disciples to "watch" for the hour of His coming.[128] Jesus then urged His disciples to "...watch therefore, for you do not know what hour your Lord is coming. But know this, that if the master of the house had known what hour the thief would come, he would have watched and not allowed his house to be broken into."[129] Jesus wants us to be ready for His coming.

At the time of Christ's coming, it will be like the days of Noah when people will be marrying and feasting. It will be normal, like any other day, but we have to stay alert and observe what is going on around

127   Nehemiah 2
128   Matthew 24:42
129   Matthew 24:42-43

us. We need to consider if we are moving towards God and gaining treasures for eternity or is everything we are doing going to pass away when He comes? We have to prepare so our future generations become and stay ready as a bride waiting for her groom.

It's not a surprise that Paul was in weariness and painfulness, in **watchings often**, in hunger and thirst, in **fastings often**, in cold and nakedness, while having a deep concern for all the churches.[130] Following Jesus is not easy and having faith in Him takes perseverance. Even Peter saw the importance to be well balanced (temperate, sober minded), vigilant, and cautious at all times; for that enemy of ours, the devil, roams around like a lion roaring [in fierce hunger], seeking someone to seize upon and devour.[131]

We do not want to be like the people who go into captivity because of their lack of knowledge, nor should our glory die of hunger or become dried up of thirst. We must know that in all seasons we need to learn to adjust to our surroundings and become ready. "Therefore, thus says the Lord Jehovah: Lo, My servants do eat, and ye do hunger, Lo, My servants do drink, and ye do thirst, Lo, My servants rejoice, and ye are ashamed."[132] We are to know this will be expected of us, as we are servants of the Lord. God has called us to be watchful and protect our kingdom family. It takes an act of faith to respond in obedience to God.

If my people, which are called by my name, shall **humble** **themselves**, *and* **pray***, and* **seek** *my face, and* **turn** *from their wicked ways; then will I hear from heaven, and will*

---

130   2 Corinthians 11:27
131   1 Peter 5:8
132   Isaiah 65:13 [KJV]

forgive their sin, and will heal their land.

2 Chronicles 7:14

God reacts to our act of obedience when we humble ourselves and pray and seek the face of the Lord. It takes faith to turn from our wicked ways, knowing it only brings destruction. We trust God has something better for us. When we do this, then God will hear from heaven and forgive us and heal our land. We can be like Nehemiah who helped rebuild the wall and became watchful of his enemies. God restored their land. It is possible, as God has purposed His plans for us in our hearts to live out victorious lives.

While you live out your faith, you will experience people who still have differences of opinion in many matters. If we get into a situation where we realize our opinion is to be ripped apart, we can remember to "...avoid foolish and ignorant disputes, knowing that they only generate strife."[133] We may say, "Let's agree to disagree," so we may end the conversation before it gets worse. It may be the best thing to do if already caught in a dispute. I felt convicted one day when I was talking to a friend about the presidential election. We saw our president differently, and it was bringing strife between us. It is much better to keep a friendship and not worry about convincing others to think like we do, when this only brings division among friends.

We are Called to Be Peacemakers

At times, to be a *peacemaker* means holding our opinions because at the end of the day, God will still do His will through and in whom He

---

133   2 Timothy 2:23

chooses. I had to repent and apologize to my friend, and thankfully, there were no offenses. But that is how easy strife can develop in a friendship.

> *To be a servant of the Lord, we are called to not quarrel but be gentle to all, able to teach, patient, and in humility correcting those who are in opposition, if God perhaps will grant them repentance, so that they may know the truth, and that they may come to their senses and escape the snare of the devil, having been taken captive by him to do his will.*
> 2 Timothy 2:24-26

If we are not doing the will of the Father, then we are doing the will of the devil. But if we are not correcting those in humility, then we are doing it in pride, and that too, is the will of the enemy.

Escaping the Snare

God wants us to know how to escape the snare of the devil, by accepting His truth and repenting for our way of thinking. God already knows what's in our hearts, but it's up to us to choose to do things His way. There is a sense of power when we confess our weakness and hand it over to God so He can remove the scales from our eyes and show us things from His perspective. This does not happen in pride or arrogance. Instead, He will give us over to our pride and arrogance and let us eat the fruit of it. There is no fruit in it, so wouldn't it be better to humble ourselves than to think we know what is best for ourselves or others?

Repentance is the key that starts our faith. It turns the ignition and enables us to start living it out. We must know that our way has not been the best or God's way. To have an attitude of repentance, is to confess our sins daily because every day we see, do, speak, hear, and think things that do not represent the goodness of our Father.

There are many ways we might fail to recognize God throughout our day. We might not become watchful of what He's doing and may tend to think that life is all about *us*. Remember, we have to become so disciplined in our bodies that we rule over them and subject them to Christ. Many of us do not rule our bodies because of a lack of self-control. If we fail a test in school, is it because the test was hard or because we didn't study for the test? When we give up is it because the task is hard or is it we aren't willing to give our best? What if we discipline our bodies to the point we accomplish what we want to in life? What would it look like if we gave all our energy to study for the test, complete a task, or do our very best? Where would we be, or what would we have already accomplished? There are many ways to motivate ourselves to do something different and create change in our lives.

Fasting

I have found going on a fast is the best way to rule over my body. I've already mentioned is hard for me to control myself with food. Since I love food, there probably comes the point when eating is no longer beneficial, especially, when I eat for the wrong reasons (such as eating mindlessly or emotionally). I may eat because I'm bored, or because food is right in front of me. I might eat because nobody else wants the food, my husband is eating it, or I think it will make me feel better. These are all poor reasons to eat, but with these, I fail daily.

149

Since I was little, I've struggled with eating too much. I remember at one point I made myself throw up after I ate, in the hope that I would not gain weight. In 8th grade, I stopped eating meat because I convinced myself that it was bad for me. I was never much of a 'sweets' person until I got older. Now over ten years later, it still matters what I consume, but I have found that fasting is a regular part of my life to help me maintain my bodyweight. Obviously, when we fast it should be to draw closer to the Lord, but there are health benefits as well.

Sometimes, we do things because we want to receive the benefits. When we pray and do not see our prayers answered, we get discouraged and question if God even heard. With fasting, we can be assured we are getting God's attention. The result may not be what you want right away, because at first fasting is hard. You will get a headache, feel weak, or feel tingling or pains. But what you will notice when you pray on your fast is that you will have clarity in your mind. You will pray powerful prayers.

Denying your flesh will give you strength in the spirit. Just as young lions lack and suffer hunger, you too shall know how that feels. How can we withstand the wiles of the enemy if we do not know how to suffer in all things? Why not train to be content even when we have more than enough? If we do this, then when disaster strikes, we will know ourselves well enough to know how long we may be able to endure. Fasting is doing things differently than pursuing fleshly desires, which is doing as you will (such as wanting to be a skinnier self). Fasting moves you from what you want to do to what He wants. His fast is to loose the bonds of wickedness, undo the heavy burdens, set the oppressed free, and break every yoke of the enemy.

Is not this the fast that I choose: to loose the bonds of wickedness, to undo the straps of the yoke, to let the oppressed go free, and to break every yoke?

Is it not to share your bread with the hungry and bring the homeless poor into your house; when you see the naked, to cover him and not to hide from your flesh?

Isaiah 58:6-7

A *yoke* is a bond between two parties (marriage) or being joined together. When a yoke is broken, that bond between the people or things break. When we or others are oppressed, it's not a good thing. There is something that yokes or binds us together to the oppression. We are to undo it's straps as if it's a collar or coupling holding us to the oppression. We are capable of breaking the yoke and separating from it through an interruption. Breaking the yoke causes it to become inoperative in lives, and it can happen by crushing the emotional bondage we have to the oppression.

For the oppressed to go free, we must recognize how are people oppressed? I believe everyone faces oppression, whether we realize it or not. *Oppression* can be considered *weariness, worry, distress, abuse in an unjustly way by authority,* or *experiencing hardship and difficulty.* We may be constantly oppressed, so how can we let someone go free if we do not know how to set ourselves free? When we give our control over to Jesus, and when we seek His will instead of our own, we can be set free. When we meet the needs of others and choose to carry their burdens, praying with them, giving them encouragement or hope, this can help others go free. When we are faced with a trial and remember our burden, we can empathize with others and meet them with compassion because we have also been through a difficulty that has crushed us.

Praying in the spirit and going through it with them, will give others hope that they are not alone. It will help break their yoke and set them free. How often have we passed by someone homeless or were quick to judge what someone was eating? Have we ever considered they may not have the funds to eat and are doing their best in life? Could it be they asked for help out of desperation? Some people are not in need but ask for help because they are greedy, but that is for God to judge. We must not assume that we know their story just by looking at them. None of us know until it's revealed whether God tells us or not, we must consider helping others because He says, "... what you have done for the least of these, you have done for Me."[134]

When we assume to know someone's life, we are letting pride win in our hearts because we're playing god by coming up with reasons why someone should not receive a blessing. God calls us to love everyone and to bless even those who curse us. The good that lives in us should be shown to the world, no matter when or where it may be. Allow God to work and mend your heart for what breaks His.

> *Examine yourselves to see whether you are in the faith; test yourselves. Do you not realize that Christ Jesus is in you-- unless, of course, you fail the test?*
> 2 Corinthians 13:5

Honestly, I fail God daily in this area. When I see someone who is homeless sometimes I shy away from giving to him or her because

---

134   Matthew 25:45

I think about what I don't have. I look in my car and realize I don't have any cash or any bottled drinks to give. I sometimes do not allow myself to get uncomfortable or allow God to work in my heart by trying to meet someone else's needs, even though previously in my walk with God, my first concern was the homeless.

When I think life is all about me, I become more selfish and look at what I don't have rather than what I do have, and I don't allow God to work in softening my heart. I have to be willing to adjust my desires to see what God is doing and join myself in His work.

I remember one day I saw a lady without shoes on her feet,
but I was not willing to take off my shoes to give them to her.
At that moment, I was thinking about myself
and did not think otherwise until I got home
and realized that I should have given
her my shoes. What stopped me?
Pride, selfishness, and lack of compassion.

"The next time," I told myself, "I will give someone my shoes."
Later, I saw a woman who was half-naked in the cold,
who I presumed needed a jacket.
I was driving in my car, and saw her from a distance.
I reasoned I would need to get out of my car
and walk where she was or drive to her.
Again, I was not willing to make myself uncomfortable.
Instead, I yelled to her and asked if she wanted a jacket.
But she kept walking past. Scripture was brought to
mind when I got home.
I failed again.

Remember when Adam and Eve hid their flesh from God? They covered themselves with fig leaves because of their own shame and guilt. They were able to know both good and evil. God has given us the ability to discern between good and evil. When we don't choose to do good, we tend to hide our sin rather than going to God. For me, it was reasoning. Our minds do not rightfully tell us what to do. Instead, our minds keep us in a state of being comfortable or safe. We then must tell our minds what to do when we learn God's ways. We must tell ourselves what is *right*.

When we are unwilling to meet the needs of others, we are *hiding* our flesh from God and people. We are not allowing our flesh to participate in something God approves of, in what He calls us to do. Hiding is turning our face from God and looking for shelter in our own self-protection and safety. God looks for obedience in us to see if we are walking in faith to what He says. I can easily hide and not do the right thing, but that does not please God, I must continue to know His will and do it, for then when I do, I know I am walking in faith.

We Should Be Growing in Our Faith Daily

Faith is doing something that scares us often or trying something new that seems impossible. We should not be afraid to look different or to be strange in the eyes of our Father. Although, He is different from the world, we too should be different. I know I want to be set free from the bondage of food and from the desire to eat all the time, so fasting is what I practice, so I'm not held captive to it. An article about our bodies states:

"Our intestines and brain talk to each other via the endocrine system (hormones released into the bloodstream) and the nervous system (nerve signals triggered in the gut and transmitted to the brain, and vice versa). At the same time, out of balance fermentation can result in the formation of endotoxins, which means the bacteria in your gut form toxins that make you weak and tired. If your gut is weakened, these toxins can easily make it into your bloodstream. Besides diet, stress management is one of the most profound ways to heal your gut biome. Studies show that stress affects the brain-gut axis and can lead to decreased nutritional absorption, enzyme production, oxygenation, and blood flow to the GI tract."[135]

Control Your Belly or Your Belly Will Control You

We may think we need to eat, but sometimes, we wish we hadn't eaten at all, or not so much. We can eat without even thinking about it because we're so used to doing it. Food seems to have so much of our attention that it hinders us from listening to God. Our guts control our brains, but if we do not control our guts, then we will not gain self-control and discipline. The more we desire intimacy with God and yearn to be in His presence, the more we will abstain from food for God to work the impossible in our lives.

To gain spiritual discipline is what mature Christians should strive for. What we bind or loose on earth we bound and loosed in heaven.[136] We are held captive to what we do not loose. This means our words have the power to forbid or allow something in our lives. We can gain spiritual discipline when we repent from our sins. When we fast and pray, we practice a focused mentality to retrain our bodies

---

135   Hadhazy, A.
136   Matthew 16:19 paraphrase

to be spiritually disciplined in the Word.

You become the master of your spirit because you are denying the natural desire of your flesh. Flesh and spirit make war with each other, so we may avoid fasting, because eating is too enjoyable or comforting to us. Eating can fill a pretend 'need' that God should be fulfilling in our lives. The secret to our contentment, is found in learning how to spiritually discipline ourselves and putting our bodies under the subjection of the spirit, when we fast according to Isaiah:

> *Then your light will break out like the dawn, and you will be healed quickly. Your own righteousness will walk before you, and the Lord's glory will be your rear guard. Then you will call, and the Lord will answer; you will cry for help, and God will say, "I'm here." If you remove the yoke from among you, the finger-pointing, the wicked speech; if you open your heart to the hungry, and provide abundantly for those who are afflicted, your light will shine in the darkness, and your gloom will be like the noon.*
>
> *The Lord will guide you continually and provide for you, even in parched places. He will rescue your bones. You will be like a watered garden, like a spring of water that won't run dry.*
>
> *They will rebuild ancient ruins on your account; the foundations of generations past you will restore. You will be called Mender of Broken Walls, Restorer of Livable Streets.*
> Isaiah 58:6-12

The Spiritual Affects the Physical

When we act in obedience to the fast in Isaiah 58, it says, "...and you will be healed quickly..." Now I know some people do not believe in miraculous healings today, but many do because they have seen and witnessed them. They have tested it out in faith. Jesus did not give us the mandate to "...heal the sick, raise the dead, cleanse the lepers and to drive out demons..."[137] because it isn't for today. Jesus is the same yesterday, today and tomorrow, which means His word stands today just as it did then.

Sometimes you must surround yourself with people who believe in unusual miracles, for you to get out of your own thinking. It could be that God wants to do something inside of your heart to work in and through you. When you don't believe in miracles, it can bring discouragement and make people feel hopeless, and that is not the God we serve. Jesus Christ in us is the hope of glory. We believe because we know that without faith, it is impossible to please God, and we know that ALL things are possible to those who believe.[138]

God owns it all, has it all, and healing is who He is as Jehovah Rophe. This doesn't mean if a healing doesn't take place, God can't do it. It just means we learn how to partner with Him through it, in the belief that He can do it, despite the outcome. You may be the miracle others need when you are going through your own pain. When we want to be healed from something in our own lives or when we want something for ourselves, we can pray for others who have that same desire because it comes from our own sincere heart for God to reach

---

137   Matthew 10:8
138   Mark 9:23

our need as well. That prayer for someone else empowers your prayer life so much more because it comes from a pure heart. If you pray in bitterness and anger because you don't understand God and you don't want God to heal your friend or bless your neighbor because He hasn't done it for you yet, then be careful. Your lack of faith can discourage others and hinder people from knowing God.

We are to represent God in a healthy manner, of who He is. When we don't understand something, we humble ourselves and pray. We ask God to show us, lead us, and teach us His ways. If we aren't able to pray for others in faith, then let's be honest by letting them know they need to ask someone who has more faith in that area than we do. Since we care enough about them and understand the magnitude of faith required to be activated, I'm sure they would greatly appreciate our authenticity of letting them know. We don't have to have everything figured out, but we should be leading people to know more about Him even when we have questions ourselves.

Since the Kingdom of God is at "hand," it may be by your "hand" that someone gets healed since the Kingdom of God is inside of you. Jesus bore our iniquities on the cross, but we are still walking around with diseases, illnesses, and infirmities. We need to stand on His promises that are still true for today even though we may not exactly know how He will do them. As long as we do our part to what He says, then there is no doubt that God will adhere to His word. When we trust God and put our faith into action, we have hope that one day we will be healed, and no sickness or diseases will be on the earth. We can have hope that other generations will not be going through what we go through. Our hope should be in our prayers and declarations for what we want to see in our future generations. As we continue to pray without ceasing, our hope should grow into an unshakable faith. There are some things we cannot do in the natural that needs to be done in the spiritual.

> *For, though we walk in the flesh, we do not war according to the flesh. For the weapons of our warfare are not carnal but mighty in God for pulling down strongholds, casting down arguments and every high thing that exalts itself against the knowledge of God, bringing every thought into captivity to the obedience of Christ, and punish all disobedience when your obedience is fulfilled.*
>
> 2 Corinthians 10:1-6

Our disobedience will be annulled when our obedience is fulfilled. Every day someone is telling us what to believe, what to do, or how to act. Just like water adapts to the environment, we too adapt to ours. Every day we will face opposition, just like a turbo wave meeting a lazy river. When you learn about your body and what God has given you and come to the realization of who you are in Christ, you will know that you are more powerful than the trickery of the devil. Your body is the temple of God. If you don't take care of it, it becomes ill.

My mother was diagnosed with cancer.
It was scary to hear, being her daughter
because we tend to believe we will outlive our parents
and do not think otherwise unless a tragedy happens
or we hear unexpected news. I was concerned,
but because I know who the Father is and
what He can do, I was not worried.

I brought my prayers to God,
and when I had a thought of worry,
I would declare my trust in Him, no matter the outcome.
I knew I had to be strong for my mother.
She would tell me her concerns,
and instead of me trying to calm her down
or say my opinion in the matter,
I replied to her in a prayer to our Father.
Every time I prayed, it was exactly what she needed to hear.
She needed to feel safe, knowing that someone
was looking out for her,
cared for her, and that someone was
walking through this with her.

Sometimes we can voice our opinions, but that doesn't always make a situation better. I know God can do miraculous things through us when we put Him as our focus. To Him, we give all praise and glory. Through our prayers, He shows us who He is, even when we pray the unthinkable or doubt in our hearts. We may act like prayer is shameful, wanting to hide what we are going through, but forgetting that God tells us to confess our sins to one another so that we may be healed. Confessing our sins does not mean that we have committed sin to have gotten sick, but we openly express our confession to what is going on in our lives.

There is healing in numbers. The more people who pray for you and are in agreement, the more miracles you will see. People can rejoice in your miracle because they were part of it. It gives others hope for what you go through. God says when two or three of us gather together and make our requests known, we can come to Him with full confidence that He hears us and will answer us according to His riches and glory in Christ Jesus. He desires to hear our prayers and to ask Him for what we want, according to His will. We partner with God, not trying to convince Him of our plans, but being flexible with His. We have no idea how He wants to work things out in our lives, but we give Him the opportunity to do so. When we submit to Him and pray with compassion in our hearts, it is limitless to what God can do in and through our lives.

"Jesus had compassion and touched their eyes.
And immediately their eyes received sight,
and they followed Him."
Matthew 20:34

It was hard not being able to be with my mother
while she was going through chemotherapy.
I was in graduate school, and there was no way for me
to be able to help her. I could only do what
I thought was best, and that was to pray for her.
Fortunately, in the summer, after finding out about
the tumor and my mother going through
the first round of chemo, my husband and I
were able to make a visit to Michigan.
We prayed for her with compassion in our hearts.
We stood in a circle in the kitchen
and prayed a powerful prayer.
At the next doctor's visit, the tumor was gone.

God Healed My Mother

You may never know how long you must go through the pain, discomfort, hurt, or trial, but faith is hoping for a miracle to happen. Sometimes if we don't see the miracle, or God doesn't heal right away, or take us out of our hurt or pain, we tend to think God doesn't know what He is doing. We forget that maybe God wants to do something either inside of us or through us, instead of instantly healing us. We tend to think God should take us out of whatever we're going through rather than walking through it with Him.

God can do anything He wants, and so can we, but it won't be pretty without Him. We must learn how to humbly accept His plan even though it may be different than what we expect or want. It is best to allow God to be God and believe that He knows what's best for us. I may not understand His ways, but through this time with my mother, we became closer in our relationship like never before. I no longer look toward my mother in anger, but I have an empathetic heart towards her. I know she was a great mother and despite what I felt as a child, I know she did the best she could for me in her situation. I'm thankful to have had this moment with her because she has helped me grow in compassion for others who feel misunderstood. She is a good person and has a kind and giving heart. I wish I would have focused more on the good things than the bad as a child. I'm thankful for God restoring our relationship and giving us a brighter and happier future. Time gets restored when we trust God.

Trusting God in all our ways is vital for our faith. Our faith cannot be partial to what we invite God to do in our lives. Remember, His ways are not our ways, and sometimes we need to trust that He is even outside of 'time.' This means when it is His 'time,' what is expected to happen, will happen, regardless of what we think or do. Learning to discipline ourselves in the Word, submitting our thoughts to His and surrendering our ways with a constant renewal of our minds takes time and practice. We can do great things when we learn to trust Him in all our ways.

Disciplined Morning Time with God

Disciplining my morning time can be hard for me to do, but I know it is vital since it was in the morning that Jesus spent time with God. "And in the morning, rising up, a great while before day, he went out, and departed into a solitary place, and there prayed."[139] When you get up in the morning, what is the first thing you do?

For many years I would get up and workout
as the first thing I did, only to feel like that wasn't right
since I did not devote my time to God.
I would spend time with God when I wanted to,
after the gym, but it wasn't God's time.

When I fail to meet God in His hour
and do it when I want to, instead,
I can miss an opportunity to hear from Him.
I might be unable to recognize
His voice because of the busyness of my day
and the consuming thoughts
that happen in my mind.

---

139   Mark 1:35

Without accountability and trusting God fully,
I can doubt if God will speak to me.
This keeps me stuck in my continued cycle
of not spending time with Him in the morning.
I realize I need Him more in my life, everyday.

When we continue to do things our way, we are missing out on what God wants to speak to us. It doesn't mean He won't talk to us, but I am sure there is a time He wants to meet with us, and it is in the morning. We can control our bodies through discipline. Our bodies control us when we do not do the right thing. Temptation is when we want to do the right thing, but it is hard to do, like waking up early in the morning. Honestly, I am still struggling with being disciplined in this area.

Even now we might try to force ourselves to sleep at night, not understanding why we can't sleep a full eight hours or why we can't get to sleep at all. As a culture, we fail to look at history and sleeping patterns to see if this is how it always was, or is there another way?

"Humans slept in two four-hour blocks, which were separated by a period of wakefulness in the middle of the night lasting an hour or more. During this time some might stay in bed, pray, think about their dreams, or talk with their spouses. Others might get up and do tasks or even visit neighbors before going back to sleep." References to "first sleep" or "deep sleep" and "second sleep" or "morning sleep" abound in legal depositions, literature and other archival documents from pre-Industrial European times. Gradually, though, during the 19th century, "language changed, and references to segmented sleep fell away ... Now people call it insomnia."[140]

Fight for the Discipline and Pray for Others

We have the choice to fight for what we want, and we can get closer to God when we go through the battle to get what we want. Otherwise, if we wait for it to happen, it won't get done. Discipline is a daily practice, in which each day we can become better at it. We focus on the process, while trusting in God, because most times, we will not see the results right away. We will have to keep at it and be patient to make it to the end. This can be with anything: a business, your body, your faith, or your relationships. It takes daily work and commitment to have meaningful and lasting investments.

Imagine a competitive football game, and one team is winning 30-0 by half-time. Now the team that is winning could think, "Man, we got this in the bag," but not continue to give their full effort in the second half. They may think they have already won, so they become subconsciously complacent. To their surprise, the other team comes back with more motivation, gives their best effort, fights with every ounce of passion, and ends up winning the game. The battle in our minds says we don't need to continue the fight because we're already doing "life." We go to church every Saturday or Sunday, thinking there isn't more we can do since we serve in the church and tend to our families and work.

---

140   Wolchover, Natalie

We already think we are doing God's divine plan for us, but are we really? To overcome the complacency, we need a driving force inside of us, knowing that this is for the glory of God. We know our purpose when we are doing it in love for Him. To continue to the end takes patience with ourselves, knowing that is where He wants us to be. It takes time but with perseverance and fight we can go all the way to the end and live more abundant lives. God loves those who are faithful in the small things, doing the daily consistencies. He loves those who keep His word. Being faithful in that, God will surely give grace and bless us if it is according to His will and for His purpose. We must remember to wait on the Lord, keep His ways and He will exalt us to inherit the land He has promised.

When We Patiently Endure, We Will Receive the Promise

"Hope deferred makes the heart sick,
but when the desire comes, it is a tree of life."
Proverbs 13:12

We have hope for what is laid out before us. Our hope in Jesus to keep His promises is an anchor of our souls, both sure and steadfast. God spoke promises to Abraham saying, "Surely blessing I will bless thee, and multiplying I will multiply thee."[141] Our hope is only found in Him. Nothing can restore us more than our confidence in Him.

When we use God's Word like medicine, it will heal our souls and renew our minds. It has the power to give others hope and faith. Faith comes by hearing the Word of God.[142] This means someone must speak about their faith. Hearing the Word gives people a deep

141   Hebrews 6:13-19
142   Romans 10:17

desire that will grow inside of them. A desire accomplished is sweet to the soul, but it is an abomination to fools to depart from evil.[143]

God gives us dreams and goals to use for His good name since they are the gifts He gives. He made us to accomplish what He has called us to do. It is sweet to our souls that we accomplish them. It is His gift to us. We can be assured that nothing good comes from evil. May our hearts be filled knowing He has a hope and future for our lives!

Hold on to God's Promises

"Though your beginning was small,
Yet your latter end would increase abundantly."
Job 8:7

When you train your body on the treadmill or in a sport, you must learn how to be a good finisher. If you give up before you accomplish your goal or before the game is over, you have cheated yourself of a possible win or achievement. You can let the whole team down by your unbelief of not winning or achieving greatness. When you give up before your finish, you are allowing the will of the enemy to settle into your heart that tells you that you are not purposed for abundance.

This allows complacency to settle in your heart. Stay diligent, persistent, and committed that you are destined for more, reminding yourself that God will finish the good work He started in you through your belief in Him. Believe He is bringing you to completion in Him. You never know whose dream is attached to yours. This doesn't

---

143   Proverbs 13:19

just apply to your teammates, but family members and society too. When we realize it's not just about *us*, but about creating a culture or nation that supports each other and truly sees each person's value, this sets us up for success. Celebrating and honoring each other gives us an opportunity to serve one another and humble ourselves. Fill your mouth with **His daily bread** more than anything else:

> *In the meantime, His disciples urged Him, saying, "Rabbi, eat." But He said to them, "I have food to eat of which you do not know." Therefore the disciples said to one another, "Has anyone brought Him anything to eat?" Jesus said to them, "**My food is to do the will of Him who sent Me, and to finish His work.**"*
> John 4:31-34

God takes care of our needs, and even the animals and birds in the air and creatures in the sea. There is not one that is displaced on earth. There have been many research studies of wild animals healing themselves, and knowing the foods to eat to induce labor. Wild animals use plants, seeds, roots, leaves, and minerals to heal their bodies and treat ailments. Even fasting is part of the healing process.

It's normal to go through hunger pains, yet most people do not want to experience it. We would rather do what makes us feel comfortable and shun all things that lead to pain but even Jesus fasted. Scientists have found that the human body cannot fast more than 40 days, or the body starts to eat itself. I have found people who had fasted 21 days without food and fasted ten days every quarter of the year. Want to receive blessings from the Lord? Then fast, *His way.*

*"When thou fastest appear not unto men to fast, but unto thy Father which is in secret: and thy Father, which seeth in secret, **shall award thee openly.**"*
Matthew 6:17-18

We may never know precisely how the Lord will bless us openly, but we can know it will come, since it is a promise, He gives us when we do it *His way*. For us to do things His way, we must know how we are operating. Our choices in life are either based on fear or out of love. We can become fearful and believe that God does not have a plan for our lives. This may cause us to do everything within our power to take control and do it ourselves, or we can give more abundantly because we know everything belongs to Him and He is not short of His supply. This way we operate without scarcity, knowing we can do things out of love because we know we are being taken care of.

Esther did not have confidence in the flesh (herself) but denied herself, prayed and fasted, and then she became bold (confident in the Lord) when she went to her king. Esther was able to face her fear because of the love she had for her people. Her love enabled her to overcome her fear of possible death and it gave her boldness and confidence in her God. Her story is remembered during the Passover. Esther fasted and prayed for three days; her fasting consisted of no food or water. How bad do you want what you are asking? Are you willing to pay such a price to deny yourself and seek after the things of God? We must believe that He is God and a rewarder of those who diligently seek Him.[144]

---

144   Hebrews 11:6

Life is in the Blood

Life in the blood is figurative and literal. Jesus' blood gave us life to live out a life that glorifies Him. We are no longer held in bondage because of sin, but we are now seen in righteousness because of His blood. We are now set free from all sickness and disease. We have the choice to believe His truth or the world's facts. Facts do not mean they are truths. Faith is our truth. Truth has a name, and He is Jesus Christ. It is by the blood that we are whole, justified, sanctified, and clean. It is through the blood that we receive an everlasting covenant of His mercy and grace.

God had prepared a body for Christ. The Church is that body. He took away the sacrifice, offerings, and burnt offerings so that His coming may be established. By Christ, we have been sanctified through the offering of His body. His flesh is the veil we enter through His blood. A veil covers to hide something. Jesus' flesh being the veil, covers us (our sins, transgressions, and iniquities). Since His body was given up for us, we can symbolically picture a veil as his body, so we can understand it covers our sin. He gave up His life/body for us when we accept and receive Him as our Lord and Savior. We have the boldness to enter the Holiest by the blood of Jesus[145] with prayers, requests, and questions because of what He has done for us.

> *But He was wounded for our transgressions, He was bruised for our iniquities; The chastisement for our peace was upon Him, And by His stripes, we are healed.*
> Isaiah 53:5

---

145   Hebrews 10 paraphrased

By His Stripes, We are Healed

God's Word does not say we *were* healed, but we *are* healed. We stand on His truth not the truth of man, feelings, or any other thing that is against the knowledge of God. We live by faith and believe God and His Word.

> *For the love of Christ constrains; us because we thus judge, that if one died for all, then were all dead: that he died for all, that they which live should not henceforth live unto themselves, but unto him which died for them, and rose again. Therefore, we know no one after the flesh from now on. Even though we have known Christ after the flesh, yet now we know him so no more.*
>
> 2 Corinthians 5:14-16

We do not know Christ anymore as a man, but now as a King on the throne. We know Him as someone who makes intercession for us,[146] as the Mediator between us and our Father,[147] of the New Covenant,[148] as the Reconciler between all things,[149] as our Judge,[150] and as the Word.[151] He is the beginning and the end, the Alpha and Omega and one day He is coming in the clouds, and every eye will see Him, even they who pierced Him. And all the tribes of the earth will mourn because of Him.[152] God is the perfect giver of our lives. He gave us His Son Jesus as a gift. Do you think He will provide something bad for you?

146	Romans 8:34
147	1 Timothy 2:5
148	Hebrews 12:24
149	2 Corinthians 5:18
150	1 Timothy 4:1
151	John 1:14
152	Revelation 1:7

Every good gift and every perfect gift is from above and comes down from the Father of lights, with whom there is no variation or shadow of turning.

James 1:17

The young lions do lack and suffer hunger: but they that seek the LORD shall not want any good thing.[153] This means those who seek the Lord already have every good thing. Can you imagine not being in want? I continuously want new things all the time: new clothes, the latest gadgets, new journals, new books, and fresh food. There are many new things that we want. Yet, could we be living as though we are not in want even though we think we may be?

For instance, imagine your children wanting new spring clothes but they just received winter clothes, are they still in need? They have what they need but because they want spring clothes, do you think the Lord will provide them? What if you do not give them the clothes right away? Do you think they will be grateful when it's a few weeks later? Would it be okay for them not to get them right away? Now imagine you are the child, wanting something from your Father. In hindsight, you may not feel like you have everything you need. Sometimes, going without something for a little while will help you appreciate it when you receive it.

However, the Bible states that those who seek the Lord shall not *want* any good thing. That means all the good things are already ours. The **Lord blesses us with every good and perfect gift,** and that means even saying, "No" or being silent could perhaps mean, "Not in this moment but possibly at a later time." God is not impatient.

---

153   Psalm 34:10

He enjoys the process of things because it's like something is always being created like the transition of a butterfly. We may not see how waiting, discomfort, or friction edifies us, but God does. We may not understand why not *right* now, but God does.

We Have a Loving Father

Our Father doesn't mind being patient and waiting for us to come to repentance in our thinking and actions. His loving kindness draws us into fellowship with Him. He is long-suffering in His patience with us. We tend to be impatient with Him because we haven't learned the beauty of waiting or slowing down. We live in a *now* society that seems overwhelmed and full of anxiety, no matter where we go. We adapt to this sort of behavior as normal in our lives. We fail to do something different because we don't see anything else being done. We can lose sight of God because we aren't patient enough to listen to Him. We can put everything into our own hands, as our own gods and sadly, think this is what life is.

> *"The work of righteousness shall be peace;*
> *and the effect of righteousness,*
> *quietness and assurance forever."*
> Isaiah 32:17

Work out your salvation. Work in righteousness. It all involves movement. We cannot obtain peace without righteousness. You will know when you have quietness when you do not complain, worry, or doubt. *Quietness* is an assurance that you are living a righteous life. Think about it. If you are not involved in gossip, slander, or contention (among other sins), then "drama" will not come looking for you. You will have learned to master the art of being righteous. It is something that we can obtain today, instead of reducing ourselves to a lower standard because we do not want to be responsible or accountable.

Assurance forever means guaranteeing you are secure in eternity with the Lord. Righteousness is life, and in its pathway, there is no death.[154] When we return to the Lord, He will have compassion on us.[155] When we seek Him while He may be found and call upon Him when He is near,[156] He will be gracious toward us. To obtain righteousness, it must be pursued.[157]

We will know we have righteousness when we are at peace even when everything comes against us. The result of righteousness is quietness and trust forever.[158] If you don't have this kind of relationship with God right now, there is a good chance righteousness still needs to be pursued. Remember, worry, frustrations, nervousness, anxiety, complaining, and discouragement, are all a foreign state to a healthy body. We can boast in our infirmities and understand the work that still needs to be done in our hearts and how Christ has worked it all out. It's the process of dying to ourselves and knowing we can't get to where God wants us to be without His help.

Righteousness will stand forever, and His salvation to all generations.[159] This is why it is good to withstand the trials and not to give up. We are pressing through not just for *us* but for future

---

154   Proverbs 12:28
155   Isaiah 55:7-9
156   Isaiah 55:6
157   Isaiah 51:8
158   Isaiah 32:17 paraphrased
159   Isaiah 51:8

generations to come! Our salvation becomes perfect through suffering.[160] Christ learned obedience through the things He suffered. When we detour from God to do things our way, it may be because we are afraid of the conflict or suffering. We do not want to feel pain and presume it's because God doesn't love us. However, God's way allows us to learn how to become obedient to Him in our suffering, pain, or discomfort. To put God first in our daily lives, is to become obedient to what He wants done in and through us. We cannot learn obedience without having suffered or getting off track. Did you know it was an abomination for kings to commit wickedness? The king's throne is established by righteousness.[161]

We are Kings and Queens

Jesus loved us and washed us from our sins in His own blood and made us kings and priests to His God and Father. To Him *be* glory and dominion forever and ever.[162] It's about time we acted like it. Wickedness should have no part in our minds, bodies, or souls. Kings have dominion and power that should not be misused or misrepresented but be represented as the glory of God. In our marriages, as queens to our kings, we represent the glory of man in which we can influence our husband's agenda. It is good to do good to our husbands all the days of our lives, with the right intent always in our hearts, not out of selfish ambition. We can learn how we willingly submit ourselves to God's order, and our husband's suggestions and ideas, as it pertains to the will of God (I am not talking about any abuse). This allows God to do a good work in our husbands that aligns us to God's will for our marriage and lineage.

---

160   Hebrews 2:10
161   Proverbs 16:12
162   Revelation 1:5-6

Righteousness exalts a nation: but sin is a reproach to any people.[163]

We Never Realize How Our Own Sin Affects Others

When we sin, we aren't just sinning against the Lord, but we are causing others to sin. Teachers will be held to a higher standard because they are to teach the way of the Lord correctly. They are not to misguide others to sin. How do you know if who you are listening to is in right fellowship with God? Listen to their speech. Is it intended to draw you near to them, or does it bring you closer to the Lord? Tolerance and compassion are two different things. We can have compassion for others for what they go through, and grow in empathy with an understanding heart, but tolerance for sin is not okay. God says to hate what He hates because if we don't, then we are tolerating sin.

What Fear are We Operating?

What is preventing us from fully surrendering to God? Is it fear of rejection, fear of not being liked, fear of a demotion in a job or career, fear of missing out, fear of not being known, fear of being known, fear of making a mistake, fear of failure or success, fear of failing the family or not being good enough.

It could be anything, but God wants us to get to the core of what is preventing us from being fully surrendered to Him and *all in for His will* on earth. We know as Christians that God is a God of order, justice, and grace. When we seek to have righteousness in our lives, He aligns our bodies to be in spiritual alignment with Himself. When

---

163   Proverbs 14:34

we are out of alignment, we develop ailments which warn us to seek and put God first in our daily lives. God chooses to bless us with so much more. Look at the promise in Proverbs 21:

He that followeth after righteousness and mercy findeth life, righteousness, and honor.
Proverbs 21:21

What a promise! Do you want honor, life, and righteousness? I know I do!

*I am the Lord your God, Who teaches you to **profit**, Who **leads** you by the way you should go, Oh that you had heeded My commandments! **Then** your peace would have been like a river, and your righteousness like the waves of the sea. Your descendants also would have been like the sand, and the offspring of your body like the grain of the grains of the sand; His name would not have been cut off nor destroyed from before Me.*
Isaiah 48:17-19

Nevertheless, the solid foundation of God stands, having this seal: "The Lord knows those who are His... Let everyone who names the name of Christ depart from *iniquity.*"[164] Do you want to belong to the household of God? Depart from iniquity; it's a choice. We must know the difference between good and evil. If we do not know what iniquity is, how can we choose to depart from it? Therefore, we must study God's Word. It is the very Word from God. We must believe it is given by divine inspiration and is profitable for instruction,

---

164   2 Timothy 2:19

for conviction of sin, for correction of error and restoration to obedience, for training in righteousness learning to live in conformity to God's will, both publicly and privately — behaving honorably with personal integrity and moral courage; so that the man of God may be complete *and* proficient, outfitted *and* thoroughly equipped for every good work.[165]

Remember that in a great house there are not only vessels of gold and silver, but also of wood and clay, some for honor and some for dishonor. Therefore, if anyone cleanses himself from the latter, he will be a vessel for honor, sanctified and useful for the Master, *prepared* for every good work.[166]

Equipped for Every Good Work

Not only does God want to prepare us, but He also equips us for every good work. He is thorough in what He wants to accomplish in and through our lives. Myles Munroe stated, "Don't measure your worth by your dirt." The word *human* is made up of *humas* and *man*. *Humas* means *dirt* and the word *man* means *spirit*, which means we are spirit and have a dirt body. God is able to mold us and shape us into the vessel He has designed and made us to be by using our circumstances to get us there. Just imagine how He has crafted us in His hands. He gave us shape, just like making of a vase from clay. With His loving touch, He formed us. We are His workmanship. John Wesley stated, "It seems without God man cannot, without man, God will not." On earth, man can do nothing without God, but God will do nothing on earth without man.

---

165   2 Timothy 3:16-17 [AMP]
166   2 Timothy 2:20-21

When we work, we are doing work unto the Lord, not for ourselves.

> *Thus says the LORD, The Holy One of Israel, and his Maker:*
> *'Ask Me of things to come concerning My sons; And concerning*
> *the work of My hands, you command Me. I have made the*
> *earth and created man on it. I—My hands—stretched out*
> *the heavens, and all their host I have commanded.'*
> Isaiah 45:11-12

There is coming a day to see if what we have done for Him was out of a pure heart or out of a deceitful heart.

> *Every man's work shall be made manifest: for the day shall*
> *declare it, because it shall be revealed by fire; and the fire*
> *shall try every man's work of what sort it is.*
> 1 Corinthians 3:13

We are not of ourselves, for since we received Christ into our lives, we now do things out of obedience to God, using our bodies as a living sacrifice to the One who gave us all things. Just as He has crafted us, shaped us, molded us, framed us, and perfected us, so shall we also use our hands to give Him thanks in all we say and do.

> *"Lift up your hands in the sanctuary*
> *and bless the LORD."*
> Psalms 134:2

When we lift our hands to the Lord, we are declaring, "Holy are You, Lord." This means God has given you **holy hands**. "I desire, therefore that the men pray everywhere, lifting up *holy hands,* without wrath and doubting."[167] Our holy hands are also good for healing. "Jesus *had compassion* and *touched* their eyes and immediately their eyes received sight, and they followed Him."[168] Scripture also states, "Paul had laid hands on them, the Holy Spirit came upon them, and they spoke with tongues and prophesied."[169] Yet, we may misuse our hands for our purposes which do not honor God with what He has given us. Our hands are not made to be used for violence in any way.

Many times, people misquote scripture to fit what they would like it to mean without finding the true meaning, such as the word *rod*. *Rod* has four different definitions in the Hebrew, however, we will look at the meaning in Proverbs 13 and Psalm 23. Proverbs 13:24 states, "He that spareth his rod hateth his son, but he that loveth him chasteneth him betimes." The Hebrew word that is used in this scripture is *Shabbat*, which means: *the rod used by a shepherd caring for the sheep*. This is the same word used in Psalm 23, "...thy rod and thy staff comfort me." As we look at both scriptures, we can understand that since it is the same word used in both scriptures, it has the same meaning. If we were to assume the word is used literally, *sparing the rod* can appear to be violent. However, if it was used literally, how is it used to mean comfort in Psalms? Therefore, we cannot assume we must discipline our children through a belt, hands, or any material thing but instead let's think about what a rod does to understand its meaning. A rod guides the sheep; it is a symbol of the shepherd's guardianship of the sheep.

---

167   1 Timothy 2:8
168   Matthew 20:34
169   Acts 19:6

"I am the good shepherd.
The good shepherd gives His life for the sheep."
John 10:11

When we are guardians over our children, we show them the way
they should go just like leading sheep where they need to be. We don't
forcefully hit the sheep to get what we want, but the rod allows the
sheep to see where we are going, pointing and leading in the right
direction. Shepherds use the rod with accuracy showing the sheep
where to go, and it can be used to stop an intruder by protecting the
sheep from any attacks. As Jesus, our shepherd, does this when He
prays and intercedes for us to our Father.

"As the Father knows Me, even so, I know the Father; and
I lay down My life for the sheep."
John 10:15

The rod gives instruction, just as we are to listen to God and obey
His voice. The way that we react to our kids has more to do with us
and how we are feeling than with what the kids actually do. This also
applies to our spouses and those we deal with at work or any contact
we have with people. We are to use our holy hands to bless the Lord's
name, as it states, "Thus I will bless You while I live; I will *lift up my*
hands in Your name."[170] We are to lift up our hands towards His holy
sanctuary (heaven). "Hear the voice of my supplications, when I cry
to You, when I l*ift up my hands* toward Your holy sanctuary."[171] We are
to lift our hands toward His commandments, "*My hands also I will*
lift up to Your commandments, which I love and I will meditate on

---

170   Psalm 63:4
171   Psalm 28:2

Your statutes."[172] The rod leads us to Jesus, the door, just as it shows where the sheep should *enter*.

> **"I am the door.** *If anyone enters by Me,*
> *he will be saved, and will go in and out*
> *and find pasture."*
> John 10:9

> *"For thus says the LORD,*
> *Who created the heavens,*
> *Who is God,*
> *Who formed the earth and made it,*
> *Who has established it,*
> *Who did not create it in vain,*
> *Who formed it to be inhabited:*
> *"I am the LORD, and there is no other.*
> *I have not spoken in secret,*
> *In a dark place of the earth;*
> *I did not say to the seed of Jacob,*
> *'Seek Me in vain';*
> *I, the LORD, speak righteousness,*
> *I declare things that are right."*
> Isaiah 45:18-19

---

172   Psalm 119: 48

CHAPTER THREE

SOUL

YOUR **SOUL** MATTERS TO GOD

*"And the LORD God formed man of the dust of the ground,
and breathed into his nostrils the breath of life;
and man became a **living soul**."*

Genesis 2:7

We are souls who live in an earthly body. It is said that our emotions are one-third of our soul. What we hear, touch, taste, see, feel enters our souls. It makes deposits into our hearts, causing seeds to take root in our bodies. Once these seeds take root, we *think* based on what has been deposited into our hearts. What we *think grows* into understanding and becomes our perceptions. Then we act upon what we have sown because of the things we have experienced through what we have watched (television, video games, movies, or books), what we have heard (by you or someone else), or what we have tasted, or felt. Our brains gather the information to make sense of what we experience but they do not necessarily make "true" or "right" perceptions. Our perceptions are based on what we believe to be "true." If we have watched something, or someone has explained something in a certain way, or if we have used our senses and validated other information, we presume the information to be "true." We can change our brains and our old habits by deciding what is true, false, and questionable.

When we sin, we do it against our souls. We are meant to protect our souls, which is guarding our hearts. We can save and restore souls. We can sow the right things into our hearts, learning these things from God's written word. This ability is why it's so important to read, study, and meditate daily on the Holy Bible. "Man shall not live by bread alone, but by every word that proceeds from the mouth of God."[173] Everything from what we say to what we do comes from our soul. If we don't give it the right fuel (Jesus) we're not going to be able to take it to its *rightful* place.

We are to manifest Jesus in our lives. To *manifest* means *to make known who or what you represent*. We have an opportunity to show the kingdom of God inside of us *if* that is what we have been feeding our soul. Otherwise, people will see worldly things, such as corruptible talk, lust, greed, or jealousy. There is coming a time we will be judged by God. Our Father will show no partiality. He will judge us for what we have chosen. We are to live in reverent fear of Him as a foreigner on this earth. We are not redeemed with corruptible things like silver and gold but with the blood of Jesus Christ, as a lamb without blemish and spot. We are set free from sins, iniquities, and transgressions. It is by Him that we believe in the gospel, knowing God raised Him up from the dead and gave Him glory, so that our faith and hope might be in God. Our belief in Jesus leads us to our Father.

Love Fervently with a Pure Heart

To purify our souls, we obey the *truth* through the spirit, until we have a sincere love for believers in God. This is loving one another fervently, with a pure heart.

---

173   Matthew 4:4

Fervently means *passionately*. A *pure heart* means *to have no malice, treachery, or evil intent but to have honesty and sincerity*. We are feeding our soul with either life or death. There is no "in between." It is either one or the other.

> *How much life do you give your soul?*
> *How much darkness are you still*
> *allowing to corrupt your soul?*

Becoming set-apart from the world is something that should be seen in the way we speak to one another and the way we interact with each other. When we learn that God wants us to get rid of all filthy language from our mouths, we have to openly confess our faults to Him, ask for forgiveness and then repent from that behavior. This is *His way* of cleansing us from the inside out. We act differently because we now *think* differently about how God sees us, which gives us the prompting to act in obedience to God because our lives are focusing on what pleases Him. Focusing on the road (God) keeps us set-apart.

Maturing in Christ

Filthy language should not be in our mouths when we mature in Christ. He doesn't want us to speak the way of the world. We are more than capable of having self-control if we are just willing to practice it. The hardest thing I have found is to tame the tongue. It's a small muscle but has a very strong bite if not used correctly. I bought the book, *30 Days to Taming Your Tongue,* by Deborah Smith Pegues, because I needed extra help, and I wanted to learn about all the areas in which I ought to control my tongue.

Colossians 3 instructs us on how to put to death the members of our earthly nature.

"Therefore put to death your members
which are on the earth:
fornication (immorality), uncleanness (impurity),
passion (lust), evil desire (elicit craving),
and covetousness (greed), which is idolatry
(because it seeks satisfaction in things
below (of the earth) and not above (in God).
Because of these things the wrath of
God is coming upon the sons of disobedience,
in which you yourselves once walked
when you lived in them.
But now you yourselves are to *put off* all these:
anger, wrath, malice, blasphemy,
filthy language out of your mouth.
Do not lie to one another,
since you have put off the old man
with his deeds and
have put on the new *man* who is renewed
in knowledge according to the image
of Him who created him,
where there is neither Greek nor Jew,
circumcised nor uncircumcised, barbarian,
Scythian, slave *nor* free,
but Christ *is* all and in all.
Therefore, as *the* elect of God,
holy and beloved,
put on tender mercies, kindness,
humility, meekness,
longsuffering; bearing with one another,

and forgiving one another,
if anyone has a complaint against another;
even as Christ forgave you,
so you also *must do.*
But above all these things put on love,
which is the bond of perfection.
And let the peace of God rule in your hearts,
to which also you were called in one body;
and be thankful.
Let the word of Christ dwell in you richly
in all wisdom, teaching and
admonishing one another in psalms
and hymns and spiritual songs,
singing with grace in your hearts to the Lord.
And whatever you do in word or deed,
do all in the name of the Lord Jesus,
giving thanks to God the Father
through Him."
Colossians 3:5-17

Throughout the Bible, we can see behavior is in correlation to a garment or something we wear or put on. As believers in Christ, we should be taking off our "old nature" and putting on the "new self," which is in Christ Jesus. As I am growing in my knowledge about emotions and behaviors, I think it is good to gain a more Biblical understanding of anger and lying. Our words matter to God. I realize how much work I still need to do with my words. Those who can bridle their tongue can be wise because it's the hardest thing in our bodies to control.

James teaches, "...but no human being can tame the tongue. It is a restless evil, full of deadly poison."[174] As I think about how my words can affect others, I can easily see the damage they can do between friends. Instead of talking about a problem I may have with someone directly, I can gossip about it to others which can cause contention between friends and the conversation can end up becoming unfruitful and unpleasing to God. Ephesians 5:4 states that there should there be "...no obscenity, foolish talk or coarse joking, but rather thanksgiving." That includes even rude comments about someone in a joking manner because deep down, we may be dealing with an offense and perhaps unforgiveness.

Not only does it cause damage to yourself but also to the hearer. When we share information with others and do not share it with the person you are talking about, chances are, the information should not be shared. When we listen to this type of information, we cannot assume it will not go back to the person or that this person will not talk about us. However, we can assume that when we listen to gossip, it causes division in our hearts.

So often this can happen between husband and wife. Remember to examine yourself, forgive quickly, and release it to God. "By the blessing of the upright, a city is exalted, but by the mouth of the wicked, it is torn down."[175] A house divided cannot stand. We honor God not by doing things our own way, finding our own pleasures, or speaking with *our own* words, but by speaking the truth in love. First John 1:5 states, "We know that God is light, and in Him, there is no darkness." Those cuss words are not from God. Those rude gestures are not from God. Those absurd actions are not from God. Second

174   James 3:8
175   Proverbs 11:11

Corinthians 13:5 states, "Jesus lives in you." Should we continue to walk in our own way or acknowledge Jesus living in us? We choose to walk uprightly because He has given us power, love, and a sound mind. It is by His power that we have the strength to do so. When we delight ourselves in the Lord by singing and praising and exalting Him, joy will encompass our hearts. Truly, we will experience the joy of the Lord as our strength to overcome any evil thing.

Anger is Something We Can Control

"He who is slow to anger is better than the mighty, and he who rules his spirit than he who takes a city."[176] We can rule our emotions when it comes to anger. We continuously see throughout the Bible, the Lord is "slow to anger."[177] When we demonstrate outbursts of anger, it can easily come from an attitude of hatred. Malice can be the root of anger and rage.

When I think about anger,
I think about most of my life.
I was angry and for a short season,
picked up the nickname, "Firecracker"
because I had a short fuse.
Any time I felt mistreated, disrespected, or
offended I would voice my opinion,
and get angry.
What I failed to realize was, I was hurt.
Even when I *thought* someone was talking about me,
it's an assumption that can build
an offense that leads to anger.

---

176   Proverbs 16:32
177   Psalm 103:8

Assumptions of Others are Never the Truth

Assumptions ruin relationships, and our true worth and value gets diminished in the sight of God and others. You are better than people's opinions, and you have the choice to release that from your soul, so you do not take on other people's bitterness, rage, or insecurity and turn it into your own. We are to protect what goes into our souls and release all malice and hatred to our Father, so there is no root of unforgiveness.

Unforgiveness causes more harm to us than good. When we allow ourselves to hold on to offenses, we are giving away our power to Satan and allowing him to rule in our lives because we now have given him a foothold through our sin. God does not want us to "cover" our sin (insecurities, self-hatred, or fear), but *uncover* what is hidden.

Acts tells us a story about a man named Ananias,
with his wife, Sapphira who had sold a possession.
He kept back *part* of the proceeds with his wife
also being aware *of it*,
and brought a certain part and laid *it* at the apostles' feet.

But Peter said, "Ananias, why has Satan filled your heart
to lie to the Holy Spirit
and keep back *part* of the price of the land
for yourself? While it remained, was it not your own?
And after it was sold, was it not in your own control?
Why have you conceived this thing in your heart?
You have not lied to men but to God."

Then Ananias, hearing these words, fell down
and breathed his last breath.
So great fear came upon all those who heard these things.[178]

You have a Choice

You have the choice to conceive something into your heart. That is
where it begins. The more we see unholy things, the more it affects
our souls, and eventually, it will manifest. I always saw my mother
angry. I didn't know any other emotions but anger. Eventually,
I became angry. I didn't know how to protect my heart, or how to
let bitterness go. I became someone who I didn't like, and my life
became unmanageable. We can allow Satan to fill our hearts when
we do not protect them by filling them with the Spirit of God.

The story of Ananias tells us so much. Because this is a husband
and wife, it says so much about the two of them and how God looks
at both. Ananias was the deceitful one, covetous (greedy), and a
liar. But because Sapphira had seen her husband hold part of the
proceeds, she was "covering" his sin by not telling the *truth*.

Today some wives do not *combat* the sin of their husbands. They do
not question it or say, "That is not right." We are not to lie to God
and test the Spirit. We are to stand up for God and declare our faith
to our husbands when they act out in disobedience. For instance,
what if Sapphira said to her husband, "That money belongs to the
Lord, and we are cheating Him. Don't you know what you are doing

---

178   Acts 5:3-4

is against Him? Do you not believe He will provide for our every need? Why do you do such an evil thing in His sight?" I wonder what his response would have been.

God gave Sapphira a chance to tell the truth. She did not know God was going to give her husband his last breath, and God could have easily counted her as guilty because she had known what her husband had done and was doing. But God giving her the chance to speak the truth and Sapphira deciding to lie to God demonstrates to us how it was in her heart to lie, covet, and conceal the truth.

God Gives Us Over to What is in Our Hearts

Sometimes we want the blessing more than we want God. We do things because covetousness and greed are in our hearts. Desiring more than what we have can happen to anyone, however, to combat our greed, we must resist the urge to do things apart from God. To remain faithful to Him is to be generous and satisfied with everything since everything is His.

"But my people would not listen to me;
Israel would not submit to me.
So I gave them over to their stubborn hearts
to follow their own devices."
Psalms 81:11-12 [NIV]

When we lie, we are lying to God. God knows what belongs to Him, and He knows what we are entrusting to ourselves rather than to Him. When this happens, we are saying to God that we cannot trust Him to take care of all our needs. We are believing a lie about our

Father if we do not understand the truth that says, He will meet all your needs according to the riches of His glory in Christ Jesus. If we do not believe Him in this truth, we will fall into deception, thinking we know what is best for us. We will be coveting what He gives us instead of learning how to manage and be good stewards of what He has blessed us with.

*"He makes the sun rise on both
the evil and the good and
sends rain on both
the righteous and the unrighteous.'*

Matthew 5:45

We Can Deceive Ourselves

We can deceive ourselves when we are not willing to submit to God. When we judge each other for what they have or do, we can subconsciously be telling ourselves how God made us and what He has for us, is not good enough. Then, we end up responding as though we do not have a greater purpose. Comparison steals all joy. Lying to yourself distorts trusting God. We are not meant to have any iniquity in our hearts. We are to cleanse ourselves from all unrighteousness, especially white lies.

I have had a learning experience with lying. It is easy to lie when you keep doing it, but then sooner or later, you get caught because you can't remember what the truth is. This can destroy relationships. The bottom line is the truth is always better. We may not be able to handle other people's reactions to the truth, but in good conscience and to God, telling the truth will give us the freedom in our actions.

Telling the truth will keep us from being deceived by Satan. What we say matters to God and what we do not say, matters to God. God does not lie.

> *God is not a man, that He should lie, nor a son of man, that He should repent. Has He said, and will He not do? Or has He spoken, and will He not make it good?*
> Numbers 23:19

We know that through God's spoken word, He speaks the truth. He does everything He says He will do, although He can change His mind. This doesn't mean that He lies, for nothing that comes out of Him is in defilement, for He is Holy. We too should also strive to be holy. "Be ye Holy as I am Holy."[179] To acquire a holy life, we must be mindful. What is coming out of our mouths? Is it pure, righteous, lovely, of good report and good virtue or anything praiseworthy— meditate and speak on these things?[180] There is so much hatred in the world today, let's be mindful of what glorifies our Father and be His instruments of calling people to Him by what we say and do. Let's be the standard that people need to see.

> ***Abstain*** *from **all appearance** of evil. And the very God of peace sanctify you wholly, and I pray God your whole spirit and soul and body be preserved blameless unto the coming of our Lord Jesus Christ. **Faithful** is he that calleth you, **who also will do it.***
> Thessalonians 5:22-24 [KJV]

---

179   Leviticus 11:44
180   Philippians 4:8

To *abstain* means *to restrain oneself from doing something*. It is to stop and hold yourself back. By now, we should know what evil and good are. But in case you need a refresher, evil is anything that holds itself up against the knowledge of God. To be disobedient to Christ is evil. The Hebrews' senses were to be trained in good and evil. There will be a time when the Lord will judge the people. None of us will escape judgment. That is why it is essential to have our own relationship with Him. It will not have mattered what our parents, our spouses, or anyone else did. What matters is our heart toward Him.

"The LORD shall judge the people: judge me, O LORD, according to my righteousness, and according to mine integrity *that is in me*."[181] It will matter what is in you, and what is in you will be judged. To have integrity, is to have an attitude that fears the Lord, otherwise, what kind of integrity will you have? "The highway of the upright is to depart from evil; He who keeps His way preserves his soul."[182] Our souls matter to God. The process of preserving food in our refrigerators will help us understand how to preserve our souls. Imagine your soul is something good and you want to extend its shelf-life. You need to keep it fresh if you want to use it or keep it. To preserve our souls, we are to depart from evil. How does it look to depart from evil? It is stopping your ears from hearing of bloodshed; it is shutting your eyes from seeing evil; it is despising the gain of oppression and not being partakers of bribes.[183]

What you *see* matters.

What you *listen* to matters.

And it *affects* your soul.

---

181   Psalms 7:8 [KJV]
182   Proverbs 16:17
183   Isaiah 33:15

Stopping Your Ears from Hearing of Bloodshed

What comes to mind when you read the above statement? Do you think of wars, violence, or killings of people? What happens when you hear about these things? It may make you angry, confused, or distraught. If it doesn't, it should. God creates the hearing ear.[184] It is with the spirit, or heart, that man hears what God is speaking. So, the state of the heart determines whether we hear the Word of the Lord, or not. Our hunger and thirst for the Lord establishes the state of our hearts. Although, God is a God of justice, He does not agree with us taking vengeance upon others. Some may settle in their thinking that there is no hope for those who have committed murder or imposed injustice, but that is not true.

God Even Cares for Murderers

Moses was a murderer. Paul (who use to be named Saul) murdered many people. It doesn't make it right, but that doesn't mean this is *who* they are. Moses was driven by his hurt and passion for the mistreatment of his own people, which lead to him making a poor decision. Imagine how upset Moses must have felt when he grew up in royalty, while his brethren were dealt unfairly. It isn't clear if he knew right away about being different, but I'm sure he didn't necessarily feel as though he fit in anywhere.

His new family (in our terms we may say, adopted him) gave him the best of everything to school him in his new identity as an Egyptian. I wonder how he must have felt having favor with the Egyptians yet looking different (for their skin color had noticeable differences)

---

184   Proverbs 20:12

and looking the same as the Hebrews but not being accepted by them due to his adoption into an Egyptian family. I can understand how upset Moses must have felt when he saw the Egyptian striking the Hebrew, but in our anger, we should not sin or take vengeance. When Moses heard about the bloodshed happening to his people, it only made sense to retaliate. When we do things our way, we are not considering God. It is easy for us to justify ourselves, believing we have the power to do so, based on our perceptions.

The Eyes are a Window to the Soul

God is Light; in Him, there is no darkness.

> *The lamp of the body is the eye. Therefore, when your eye is good, your whole body is also full of light. But when your eye is bad, your body also is full of darkness. Therefore take heed that the light which is in you is not darkness. If then your whole body is full of light, having no part dark, the whole body will be full of light, as when the bright shining of a lamp gives you light.*
>
> Luke 11:34

Our goal is to be like God, which is attainable if we do what He says. "The precepts of the LORD are right, giving joy to the heart. The commands of the LORD are radiant, giving light to the eyes."[185] Do you ever think about shutting your eyes from evil? It is evil to take women or children from their homes and put them into trafficking. Even watching TV shows and movies showing this, can subconsciously make you agree with it because you are allowing

---

185   Psalm 19:8

your eyes to watch it. It enters into your soul and causes it to be unclean. Anything that distorts itself from the knowledge of God, can be considered evil. It can be sexual immorality (couples having sex that are not married), watching mediums on television, going to a psychic, or hypnosis.

Second Corinthians 10:3-5 states:

> For though we walk in the flesh, we do not war after the flesh, for the weapons of our warfare are not carnal, but mighty through God to the pulling down of strongholds, casting down imaginations and every high thing that exalts itself against the knowledge of God and bringing into captivity every thought to the obedience of Christ.

Remember, our thoughts determine our actions, and they can hinder or excel where we go in life.

Submit Yourselves to God

"Resist the devil, and he will flee from you."[186] You can defeat the devil by submitting to God. You can resist the devil by not giving in to sin, and by choosing something else that is good, lovely, and pure. If someone makes you sin, do not contact that person. Take all the necessary precautions not to be tempted and fall into sin. If drinking is an issue, do not go to parties where there will be alcohol or out to bars. Do not make the decision to have "just one." Refrain from watching people drink on television or going to your friend's house who you know will have alcohol. Do everything necessary to

---

186   James 4:7

make sin difficult for you and have a plan for healthy options before the temptation comes into your mind. Wise counsel can help keep you accountable.

We are to dislike oppression. This would not be difficult for most people, but we still live in a society that oppresses people (women, race, religion, social status, economy, and so on). Men can also be oppressed because as a society we say they are to *provide* for their families, but then we (wives, exes, women) shun their thoughts or *opinions* in the home. How many men do you see in daycares or taking care of the nursery? We don't give them any place to take their mandate in the home because we may want the control, and think our way is right, and their approach is wrong. Perhaps, we do this because of our own fears. We try to "protect" our children, assuming all men may harm the babies, so we react in fear because we are afraid of abuse happening. When we don't have control over something, we are quick to think their opinion is wrong and dismiss their ideas or suggestions. I'm not saying this is happening in all situations, but it is a stigma for women and men to behave like this, thus affects the standard in society.

Oppression is living in a manner where someone else has planned something for your life. It's *like* you are being held captive or *you are* being held captive or have been tricked. Oppression can happen not just between the rich and the poor but in everyday life. Many people get into marriages and find out that their spouses are nothing like the person they thought they were. It can get messy and then we fight to take power or try to gain control as the "one" who makes the decisions in the home. We may not listen to each other or come up with a compromise because someone gets offended or defensive.

Then, marriages are left with a stigma that it is better not to marry because nobody knows how to talk assertively to one another. Instead, we try to battle it out or manipulate the situation or person. We do this because we believe we must keep ourselves "safe" and defend our "security." We think getting loud, fighting, withdrawing, and arguing is normal because that is what we have seen growing up. It has been on television, sending us subliminal messages that this is how life should be. We may experience it in our families, so we assume this is normal to get what we want.

Is it the Lifestyle God Desires for Us?

As adults, we have the responsibility over our children to make sure they grow up to be productive citizens, but without seeking God or gaining wise counsel, chances are we are taking what we saw as a child and applying what we went through with them. We may do the exact opposite out of fear because we think what our parents did wasn't the "right" way, so we go to the extreme opposite.

It can create a mess when we think and behave like *the world* and have no boundaries to what we allow our eyes to see and our ears to hear. Romans 6:3-4 puts it like this:

> *...when we were baptized into Christ Jesus, we were also baptized into His death, we were buried with Him, but just as Christ was raised from the dead by the glory of the Father, we even should walk in newness of life.*
> Romans 6:3-4

We have the choice to let sin reign in our lives or flee from it and resist the devil. We don't go towards it or let it enter our bodies whether it is watching, speaking or hearing something that does not belong to or glorify God. We have the ability from the Holy Spirit to present ourselves as being alive from the dead and being instruments of righteousness to God. When we continue to do the way of our family and not seek something new in Christ, we are continuing to allow our iniquities to be in our lineage. Iniquities are generational sins. They cannot be broken unless we decide to humble ourselves and seek God's way. He will give us a new understanding, a new way, and new hope that things can change and get better. The destination will become much more precise.

This Life is *All* for Him

Is He pleased with the choices we continue to make? Think about Jesus on the cross and what He did for us. We died to sin; let's not live in it any longer. He says we are set free from sin and have become slaves of God. We now have fruit to holiness, and everlasting life.[187]

> *Do you not know that to whom you present yourselves, slaves, to obey, you are that one's slaves whom you obey, whether of sin leading to death or of obedience leading to righteousness?*
> Romans 6:16

Does this mean that we only have two choices in whom we are serving? Absolutely! Are you obeying God, or the devil?

> *A servant of the Lord must not quarrel but be gentle to all,*

---

187   Romans 6:22 paraphrased

> *able to teach, patient, in humility correcting those who are*
> *in opposition, if God perhaps will grant them repentance,*
> *so that they may know the truth, and that they may come to*
> *their senses and escape the snare of the devil, having been*
> *taken captive by him to do his will .*
>
> 2 Timothy 2:24-26

I do not believe in the saying, "God does not give you more than you can handle." I believe He does give us more than we can handle because normally when it's about *us*, we have to continue to die to our flesh every day and in turn, that is really difficult. Many people give up because it's not easy. Many fall away because they think there has to be a *simpler* way than the truth, so they come up with their own understanding or search for other things that are not of God, not knowing they are deceived. Because of a lack of understanding, it is easy to fall away.

Those who walk righteously and speak uprightly will be able to overcome the devouring fire of others and what non-believers will go through. Do you want to remain in fellowship with God? Walk righteously and speak rightly. Work righteousness in your daily walk. Work out your faith with what is already in you. Do not be led by the desires of the flesh, for the flesh desires what is contrary to the Spirit, and the Spirit is contrary to the flesh. The flesh and Spirit conflict with each other so that you are not to do whatever you *would* do.[188] We all can have the right *intentions*, but that doesn't mean we read our Bibles and apply what we have learned or walk out our faith.

---

188   Galatians 5:17

To Become a Doer of the Word is to *Apply* the Bible to Our Lives

The Bible is for "...reproof (an expression of disapproval), correction, and instruction in righteousness. That the man of God may be perfect, thoroughly furnished unto all good work."[189] Many Christians today still speak of being a sinner saved by grace, or they say, "This is the way I've always been." They identify themselves as though it's okay to sin.

We either blame culture, experience, or our past to reason who we are today. We opt out of trying to live righteously because we would rather accept the sin in our lives. Submitting to sin doesn't represent the *gift* God has given us and it's contrary to who God says we are. I don't know about you, but I'd rather see myself as He sees me because I can easily think, "I've got God," but still do things my way. Because of His love for me, it yields me to want to change, to do things differently and not think I know best, when *clearly,* I don't.

Love ultimately conquers all. We cannot truly love ourselves if we do not know what *the meaning* is behind what we do. When I am willing to learn, remain teachable, seek, and ask for direction and keep Him as my focus, I am able to be a testimony to someone who needs to hear about Him. This keeps my faith alive as I get to see the start or boost of their faith. Sharing our faith moves us from faith to faith, as we should constantly be growing in the knowledge of Him and in our relationship with Him. When we speak about our Father, it should be out of gratitude, thankfulness, and gratefulness for all that He has done and will do in our lives. It is trusting Him, no matter how "dead" things may seem and *believing* He can make all

---

189   2 Timothy 3:16-17

things "new" or alive again.

It may be hard to keep Him as a focus when you own a business. In business, you must work at it, or else you don't see it grow. There is marketing, networking, recruitment, sales, inventory, and production that you must be mindful about. I feel as though all my days so far have been seed planting. I have no idea how the increase will come, but I do know that the increase comes from God. Since every beginning starts small, and I know one day there will be a harvest. In the meantime, I must keep working on my business. It is the same for my marriage and one day, with our children. It takes work 24/7, and to think that we should not put work into something we want, tells us something about ourselves. Whether it is fear of rejection or fear of failing or succeeding, there are many reasons why we do not face opposition and instead, decide to do what makes us feel comfortable.

When hardships come, we quickly want to believe that it is not from God. We are quick to cast it out, rebuke or pray for it to leave rather than embracing where we are. I'm not saying there are not spiritual attacks and that there are things that happen that should not happen, but instead I know God tests our hearts.[190] I know He searches to see who is fully committed to Him so He can strengthen them.[191]

Paul even learned how to be faithful in all circumstances whether in prison or out. He learned to be content whether he was full or hungry, and both in abundance and suffering need.[192] There is a

190   1 Thessalonians 2:4
191   2 Chronicles 16:9
192   Philippians 4:12

secret we must learn from Paul, which I have experienced in my own life. It is having the sufficiency of God. Whether we have many things or very little, God is the one who gives and takes away. We cannot assume that everything that happens to us is not meant to happen. But when it does happen, we ought to be prepared in our minds, knowing that the One who is Omnipotent and Omnipresent knows what is happening to us and will strengthen us in our time of need, no matter how long the season may be.

Our Father in heaven knows you. He knows what you need before you ask. It is our own selfishness He is trying to work out in us, so we have total reliance upon Him. I had to work on my self-sufficient attitude, where I thought I was good without Him. Since I believed He had forgotten me, I *convinced myself* that I could do life on my terms. This led me down a path of despair, heartbreak, and bondage. It was not easy to give up my way of thinking and behavior to do something different, but it was the loving-kindness of God that drew me into repentance. I gave up the things I loved and in turn, thought about what He cares about and did what He says to do, no matter how it made me feel. So how do you know if you are walking righteously? The effect (what you get *after* you have been walking in righteousness) will be quietness and assurance forever.[193] If you have not experienced quietness in your life, then you are not there yet, keep going.

---

193   Isaiah 32:17

Seek Peace and Pursue It

Do all that is in you to be the best *you* possible. The world will know us by our love, meaning, we should be growing in our love for each other. The world will see us treating other Christians with respect, honor, generosity, gentleness, patience, long-suffering, kindness, and will want to know our God. How are you making Jesus look attractive? Our words matter to those who are watching us. Our actions matter because people watch us. If we look like the world and sound like the world, we will not be attractive. People may think, "Why would I need your God if you do the same thing as me and are no better?" Think about who you are living for and whose you are. We have the capacity to move mountains but if we just want to be in the valley all our life without ever getting to the mountaintop than we are not living to our full potential as a Christ-follower.

I believe we can do all things
through Christ who strengthens us.
I believe God is limitless in His capacity
to help us in good and bad times.
I believe God speaks to His people uniquely
and individually as well as collectively
and gives us wisdom and understanding
of who He is and who we are.

God wants to have an intimate relationship with us, where we no longer question if He is speaking to us. We can, instead, *know* what He says is directed to us and we respond by immediately obeying Him. I believe God wants to heal all areas of our lives, even with our family members. I believe our family is our first ministry and should be treated with our utmost care. Even now, I am in the best relationship with my mother that I have ever had, and it continues to keep getting better. God is not out of reach for our families and those we love.

If ministering to your family is difficult, it may be better to start with those who are acquaintances first, as it may be less vulnerable with them than those who are closest to you, and that's okay. Do what makes you comfortable first by making amends, forgiving, and reconciling differences. I have learned that I cannot hold grudges when I'm praying for those who have hurt me. Maybe prayer is where you need to start, and in return, the rest will fall into place. Ask God if there is anyone who you would not be able to hug if you saw them and allow God to speak to you so you can forgive them in your heart.

God Cares about Your Heart

At the end of the day, it will not matter what people did to you; God will ask you what you did, not what they did. Remember, He will deal with them, but you still have a choice in the matter, and you can either let the enemy rule in your heart or choose God and do what He says, no matter how difficult it may be. I mentioned earlier, that when we choose not to forgive, we give the enemy a foothold in our hearts. It begins as a seed of deception by thinking people do not need our forgiveness or we aren't ready to forgive. It's a deception because that is not what God tells us to do.

God reminds us that He forgave us even while we were still sinners.

When we came to Him, we were not living in righteousness. In fact, all of us were *sinners*. Imagine your friend (unknowingly) sinned against you by talking behind your back and you found out about it. It would be easy to talk about your friend to that same person too because you're upset, hurt, and humiliated. But, instead of confronting your pain of being hurt by a friend, you may curse them out, take revenge or do something that hurts them, rather than talking about *how* it hurt you.

It's emotionally easier to try to gain control over the situation and try to convince someone to think 'our' way or to be on 'our side' because we want 'approval' of our perception, but it only brings more strife and division. There are many reasons why we choose to do something in our own way, but these things do not lead us closer to God.

> *"Anxiety in the heart of man causes depression,*
> *but a good word makes it glad."*
> Proverbs 12:25

When we learn about Christ, we find out how to submit unto Him by obeying what He says to do. If He says, forgive your friends 70 times 70, then that means to do it over and over again, no matter how many wrongs they have done.

> *But if we confess our sins, He will forgive our sins, because*
> *we can trust God to do what is right. He will cleanse us from*
> *all the wrong we have done.*
> 1 John 1:9 [NIV]

When we willfully chose to sin, we are choosing death, and it separates our spirit from God. To go back into communion with God, we must confess our sins, repent from our sins, and receive His forgiveness. When we believe in our hearts who Jesus says He is and confess it, we have an opportunity to show Him our belief in Him through baptism. It's an outward expression of what He has done in our lives and a faithful commitment to Him to now do things a new way. We are able to do because He gives us a new spirit. Peter replied:

> *"Repent and be baptized, every one of you, in the name of Jesus Christ for the forgiveness of your sins. And you will receive the gift of the Holy Spirit."*
> Acts 2:38

Forgiveness guarantees joy. When we truly forgive, God gives us eternal joy in our hearts. Mercy surrounds those who trust in the Lord. The Lord wants us to rejoice, be glad, and shout for joy, for He preserves us in times of trouble and provides us a hiding place in Him. He will surround us with songs of deliverance and instruct and teach us in the way we should go. In Matthew 18:23, it states, "The kingdom of heaven is like a certain king who wanted to settle accounts with his servants."

Imagine that you have an unpayable debt, one that is too much to bear. When I think of debt, I think about what I owe for my student loans: $100,000! I think about the Loan Forgiveness Program, but I don't necessarily fully trust that all my debt can be *forgiven* just through this program. I still think I owe something to them, so I feel forever indebted to my student loans. I must pay a cost every day to pay them back. I am not free with my money to spend, give or save how I would like to, until this or any other debt is paid off.

Jesus was moved with compassion when He healed us on the cross. Our debt to Him can never be repaid. Think about the cost that He died for us. He forgave us even though our sin was great. When we choose not to forgive others, we are saying, "I don't trust you, God; I will be indebted to You and hold myself in bondage from living a free life." Jesus gave us liberty. Jesus gave us freedom. Jesus has given us grace for our sin nature, our circumstances, and who we are. It's a free gift that cannot be repaid. *You are forgiven of your sins through His grace.*

We Have to Have a Spiritual Mindset

We must know that:

> *...we do not wrestle against flesh and blood (people and behaviors) but against principalities, against powers, against the rulers of the darkness of this age, against spiritual hosts of wickedness in the heavenly places (unseen places). Therefore take up the whole armor of God, that you may be able to withstand in the evil day and having done all, to stand (not shelter ourselves or hide, but stand). Gird your waist with truth (truth is in Jesus), having put on the breastplate of righteousness and having shod your feet with the preparation of the gospel of peace; above all taking the shield of faith with which you will be able to quench the fiery darts of the wicked one (we are to prepare and be ready to share our faith.*
> Ephesians 6:11–16

Having a firm foundation in our faith that is immovable when persecution comes, when hardship comes, when things seem incongruous, we have to know the reason behind it all and believe in the faith that our Lord Jesus Christ will get us through it. "All who desire to live godly in Christ Jesus will suffer persecution."[194]

Persecution is Guaranteed to Us

I'm not sure why we haven't been able to embrace this yet. I know nobody likes it, but that doesn't mean it will go away. We have to learn to deal with it, patiently and in faith. Knowing God is perfecting our faith and building us up to be partakers in His glorious kingdom. When we do this, we are manifesting the evidence of the righteous judgment of God, so we may be counted as worthy in the kingdom of God, for which we also suffer.[195] We have something beautiful and wonderful waiting for us, as long as we hold on to the hope we had when we first believed. Stand firm until the end.

Be a good finisher, not just an impressive starter.
But allow yourself to be flexible,
going with the flow
no matter how it might differ from your thoughts and
ways and wait on the Lord.
Do not be afraid of those that can harm the body
(physical attacks, verbal attacks) and
not the soul (fear God who can take our soul/life).
Accept the wrong and let yourselves be cheated.
1 Corinthians 6:7 (paraphrased)

---

194   2 Timothy 3:12
195   1 Thessalonians 4-5 paraphrased

People are people; we all are God's creation. Fear God who can take our souls with one breath. When we love God with all of our minds, hearts, souls, and strengths, we will be driven to love beyond our own capacity and through the power of God. "There is no fear in love, but perfect love casts out fear, because fear involves torment. But he who fears has not been made perfect in love."[196] When we know how much we are truly loved, we do not have to fear others or fear what we do not have. His love casts out fear in our lives, knowing that we are safe, secure, and can trust a God who has our best interests in His heart. Even when we may not feel loved or we face a fearful situation, we can decree and declare the excellence of God's love in our hearts as we set our minds on who He is and what He has done for us.

> *He looketh upon men, and **if any say,***
> *I have sinned, and perverted that which was right,*
> *and it profited me not; **He will deliver his soul** from going into*
> *the pit, and his life shall see the light. Lo,*
> *all these things worketh God oftentimes with man,*
> ***To bring back his soul** from the pit,*
> *to be enlightened with the light of the living."*
>
> Job 33:27

He will deliver our souls from going into the pit and bring them back from the pit. Some of us need to decree this over our family members and those we care about, knowing He will also do this for us. God is merciful, but do not be fooled. If we do not repent and acknowledge we are in sin and need a Savior, He has the capacity to turn us over to our sin and what is in our hearts.

---

196   1 John 4:18

As a Christian, I always hear about money and how it can cause so much harm in a person's life. It's not because money is bad, but because our hearts are bad, and we do not know how to steward money righteously. Money helps us help others, but if we don't realize we are blessed to be a blessing, then greed and covetous ways can settle into our hearts. We learn in the Bible we cannot love two masters. Either we love money, or we love God. From the depths of our hearts, we should love God. However, we do not love God when we think we should have more than someone else, compare our lives to others, or think of ways to make more money, not caring about how we obtain it, such as taking advantage of people to get it. This does not show we trust God.

In Acts, it talks about Simon believing in Jesus Christ and then by the laying of hands, he received the Holy Spirit. When he saw this, he offered Peter and John money because he wanted the power of the Holy Spirit that whenever he laid his hands on someone, they would receive the Holy Spirit as well. Peter said to him, "Your money perish with you because you thought that the gift of God could be purchased with money."[197] Now, the Holy Spirit is a free gift from God and whatever the Holy Spirit chooses to do (save, heal, deliver, teach, etc.), it is a gift from God to that person or congregation.

To Be Clean on the Inside

We have to give to the poor the things we have to be clean on the inside.[198] Give our possessions (what we own) to the poor. Otherwise, we can fall into greed and self-indulgence.[199] When we give the poor

---

197   Acts 8:20
198   Luke 11:41
199   Matthew 23:25

what we have, it helps us overcome selfish desires. God does not want us to be hoarders or covet the things we have.[200] He wants us to become wise stewards of His possessions. We can ask ourselves, "Would I be willing to leave everything behind if Jesus were to come back today?" We must acknowledge everything belongs to Him; we enter life naked, and we die naked, nothing belongs to us. Think of it as a giving rotation, when we give our personal belongings to the poor, or to the needy in the household of faith, we can trust in the promise that God will take care of our every need. We are told to not worry about what we shall eat, drink, or wear, which means God knows how to take care of those needs. What we think we need may not necessarily be a need at the moment. I remember hearing a testimony from my husband, who had a friend who needed food. He asked her, "Have you asked God yet?" and she hadn't, but that night she asked God. An hour later a lady called her phone and said God told her that she needed food. That is the God we serve! Sometimes, we are so quick and desperate to do it our way that we do not want to wait on God because we are afraid that He won't answer us.

I remember when I moved out to Vegas,
there was a month that I did not have
rent money. My car had just blown its tire,
and I was making $10/hour and getting paid
every two weeks. My checks were barely
$400 since I was working part-time.

I literally had no money to my name
because I was sharing rent

---

200   Hebrews 13:5

and still paying for my car,
and then I had creditors harassing me.
I told my dad what was happening,
but I had never asked my parents for anything.
They weren't really the types to give me anything
but maybe that is because I have always
had a job and was self-sufficient.

One night, I ran into a well-known boxer
leaving work, and he told me that he wanted
my shirt I was wearing and that he would
pay one hundred dollars for it.
Maybe it doesn't seem like a lot of money to some people,
but to me, I *needed* the money to fix my tire,
so I couldn't care less about the shirt I was wearing.
He told me that he would take me to my car.
I was walking with my roommate,
so she went with me. There was also a lady
walking with him, so I didn't think he would try
to "talk" to me because this lady looked like
she was *with* him.

He ended up taking a handful of cash
out of his pocket and told me he had $3000
and more at home and that he would like
to give it to me *if* I came home with him.
Honestly, I needed that money, but I knew
that was not what God wanted me to do.
I told him I would get back to him
and call him when I got home.
I kept thinking, what would happen *next time*
if I needed money? Would I have to go back

to this guy and get it?
I did not want to subject myself to it,
even though I was desperate.

I see how easily it could have been
for me to do it since it was money
he didn't care about and something I needed.
But instead, I laid out before God
crying before him for two days.
TWO DAYS.

Then the unexpected happened,
I got a phone call from my dad who said
he was sending me some money.
I was able to pay rent, get my tire fixed
and pay some creditors.

I would have never waited on God
if I *thought* this guy was my *only* way out
to pay for what I needed.
Instead, I poured my heart out to God,
waited, and trusted that He would get me
through it somehow. I'm thankful He worked
in my earthly father's heart to help me.
That is the God we serve!

We never know how or when God will work in our lives, but the point
is to get to the place that He is our only source of income, supplies,
food, and shelter. Think about if we trusted God for every decision,
every circumstance, and every thought? When He is quiet, is when
we might put things into our own hands, but He says the just will

live by faith. So, if the waiting causes fear and worry and we move because of doubt, most likely He didn't want us to move because we did it out of our own anxiety. If we move trusting God will go with us and be with us, chances are He will. Everything we do should stem from faith. Faith drives us to move in hope towards God.

> *"Everyone who confesses the name of the Lord must turn away from wickedness."*
> 2 Timothy 2:19

Everything is Driven by Our Thoughts

Our thoughts drive everything in our lives, and then are acted out based on what is in our hearts. To cleanse ourselves from anything that is not from God, we have to confess our wrongdoing openly. We need to confess to God even about giving our bodies to our girlfriends and boyfriends and creating a soul tie with someone due to fornication. We also can have emotional soul ties without fornication, such as friendships with people and family members.

A *soul tie* is a spiritual and/or emotional connection or connecting in sexual relations. We can see a healthy soul tie when the soul of Jonathan was knit with the soul of David because Jonathan loved him as his own soul[201] and an unhealthy soul tie was when Shechem laid with Dinah (young and unmarried) and defiled her, his soul cleaved to her.[202] God made sex to be with one man and one woman (a man will leave his family to be with his wife, and the two shall become one flesh[203] and for sex to be during the marriage.

---

201   1 Samuel 18:1
202   Genesis 34
203   Ephesians 5:31

Abstinence is not more spiritual, nor should it be practiced between a married couple, unless the couple is fasting for a short time, but then must come together soon, or they will be tempted because Satan knows how weak we are when it comes to not being intimate.

When we have sexual relations with someone who is not our spouse, we are becoming "one" with them. They have a piece of us that is a part of them, and we have a piece of them. Imagine a piece of gum getting caught in your hair; you cannot separate it without taking some of the hair; our souls work the same way. To severe the ties, we must confess our faults and speak that the ties are severed (we work through this in the *Accelerate Your Faith Workbook*). Just as God speaks and creates with His words, we speak and create life or death. We can break ties, restore generations, break curses, and restore lives.

The Power of Jesus

There is nothing we can't do without the power of Jesus. However, we must *believe*. He has given us authority to take back what the enemy has stolen from us, and we can do it through faith in the words we speak, but then we must not continue to sin willfully. We must understand why it is wrong and how it destroys our bodies, our relationships and ultimately our souls. When two become *one* through marriage, it is a covenant. It is a God-given covenant because God created marriage, and He made it for us to be in fellowship with Him in it. When we deter from the promise we made to our spouses and to God, we are not allowing God to be God in our marriage. Ultimately, we are not allowing Him to rule in our hearts for what He wants to accomplish in our marriages. When we have sex with someone outside of marriage, we are not only dishonoring God but sinning against our own bodies. When we have accepted Jesus as our Lord and Savior, we now have the Holy Spirit who lives inside of us. When we sin, we are allowing Him to be partakers in our sins when we choose to sin against Him and our bodies. Many of us were slaves to sex but now we are bought with a price. We give our bodies to Him, as holy and pure.

> *"Marriage is honorable among all,*
> *and the bed undefiled,*
> *but fornicators and adulterers*
> *God will judge."*
> Hebrews 13:3-4

We must know that when we choose to partake in sexual sin, we are choosing to not enter the kingdom of God.

> *Do not be deceived, those who practice sexual immorality will not inherit the kingdom of God: neither fornicators, nor idolaters, nor adulterers, nor effeminate, nor abusers of themselves with mankind.*
> 1 Corinthians 6:9

When we choose these things, God sees us as unrighteous. 1 Corinthians 6:10 teaches that the same goes for those who are covetous, thieves, drunkards (habitually drunk), revilers, (criticizing in an abusive or hostile way or spreading negative information about someone) and extortioners (threatening others to gain money; blackmailing). If God was to let everyone who does this into the Kingdom of Heaven then the heaven would look like earth, and there would be no need for Heaven to invade earth if it was the same. But it is not the same. In heaven, there is no unrighteousness acts; it is pure, clean, and holy. To demonstrate on earth as it is in heaven, starts with *us*. We are to be able to demonstrate our Father and His creation in a rightful manner.

> *The heart is wicked, who can conceive.*
> *"The heart is deceitful above all things,*
> *And desperately wicked;*
> *Who can know it? I, the Lord, search the heart,*
> *I test the mind, Even to give every man according to his ways,*
> *According to the fruit of his doings.*
> Jeremiah 17:9-10

"Flee also youthful lusts; but pursue righteousness, faith, love, peace with those who call on the Lord out of a pure heart."[204] "Those who cleanse themselves from the latter will be instruments for special purposes, made holy, useful to the Master and prepared to do any good work."[205] God wants us prepared. We cannot go and minister to others when we ourselves are dealing with sin.

God wants us to live good and fulfilled lives. When we guard our hearts, we are protecting them from unrighteousness, so it does not come out of our mouths, because when it comes out of our mouths, it defiles us and we know it has taken root in our hearts. We must eliminate it from our souls by speaking who we are from God's word. Jesus came so we would live life abundantly, but we cannot see the abundance if we still choose our way to live our lives.

---

204   2 Timothy 2:22
205   2 Timothy 2:21

The world has misused the word *happy*, and unknowingly, we have accepted the world's understanding of what it is to be *happy*, to the point of breaking covenants, and doing things for our own pleasures and out of selfishness. Remember the enemy comes to kill, steal, and destroy. That means he came to kill the desires and dreams God puts in our hearts, steals our inheritance from God, and destroys covenant relationships. God desires for us to be happy, but happiness is not an emotion (since we know it is fickle), but it is a *state of being*.

> *Take, my brethren, the prophets, who have spoken in the name of the Lord, for an example of **suffering, affliction, and of patience.***
>
> *Behold, we count them **happy which endure.** Ye have heard of the patience of Job, and have seen the end of the Lord; that the Lord is very compassionate and of tender mercy.*
>
> *But above all things, my brethren, swear not, neither by heaven, neither by the earth, neither by any other oath: but let your yes be yes; and your no, no; lest you fall into condemnation.*
>
> *Is any among you afflicted? Let him pray. Is any merry? Let him sing psalms.*
>
> *Is any sick among you? Let him call for the elders of the church; and let them pray over him, anointing him with oil in the name of the Lord:*
>
> *And the **prayer of faith** shall save the sick, and the Lord shall raise him up; and if he have committed sins, they shall be forgiven him. Confess your faults one to another, and*

pray one for another, that you may be healed.

The effectual fervent prayer of a righteous man availeth much.

James 5:10-16

I do not think we would consider, "...to be happy is to endure suffering, affliction and of patience." In fact, I can't think of anyone who likes to endure pain. But *happy* is he who endures these things.

Job was patient and had seen *the end* of the Lord. There is something about blessing, giving, and offerings that I think the body of Christ can grow into, especially, in the household of faith.

Therefore, as we have an opportunity, let us do good to all people, especially to those who belong to the family of believers.

Galatians 6:10

Many times, we are afraid to do anything that doesn't seem 'normal.' This can easily become idolatry. He calls us to be set apart, distinct and for His glory. When we choose to not step out in faith, it is because we would rather *people please* than be rejected. To avoid rejection, we may try to control people or manipulate them to get what we want. So often, we base who we are on how we feel. What if we have suppressed our emotions to the point we no longer know how we feel? We might try to control the situation with what we want to happen and in turn, hurt others by not having compassion or understanding toward them. Ignoring our pain doesn't mean we're not going through it. Instead, we can recognize *where* the pain is coming from, and ask what caused it? Is it from a past hurt, or is someone speaking to the rejection we felt as a child? It is a choice to surrender that pain, hurt, and/or abandonment. It is a choice to surrender the need for control or manipulation and turn it over to God.

We constantly die to ourselves by surrendering what we want and deciding to turn our hearts to Him, and He will enter our hearts by the renewing of our minds knowing He can do something different. We take a risk of being rejected rather than submitting to control or passivity. We have an abundant mercy and a heavenly inheritance.[206] We are kept by the power of God. Jesus saves us, gives us an inheritance and by His power and will, He keeps us. When we know we are safe in Him, we know we can trust Him. As the body of Christ, we should be the driving force in maintaining freedom on the earth. The body of Christ should rise up and say, "Let us return and be restored to the Lord." Instead, we might base our decisions on whether we are "happy." Aren't we tired of misusing the word *happy*?

God Desires for Us to Be Happy

"Where there is no vision, the people perish: but he that keeps the law, happy is he."
Proverbs 29:18

---

206   1 Peter 1:3-9

"Most assuredly, I say to you,
a servant is not greater than his master;
nor is he who is sent greater
than he who sent him.
If you know these things,
happy are you if you do them."
John 13:16-17

Do you have faith?
Have it to yourself before God.
Happy is he who does not condemn
himself in what he approves (when he eats).
Proverbs 14:22

When we know who we are and believe in God to the point that no matter what happens in our life we know that God is faithful and good despite what we may face or feel, then we can receive that inner peace and joy in our lives. Our joy is not dependent on our circumstances but in whom we belong. The joy of the Lord is our strength. Why is that? Because He has given us the inner strength to persevere through the sound of our praise. Our praise ignites our joy in the Lord and reminds us that He can get us through it and that He is with us in the storms. We know we can overcome our trials and pain because He has given us the gift of the Holy Spirit.

A new heart also will I give you, and a new spirit will I put
within you: and I will take away the stony heart out of your
flesh, and I will give you a heart of flesh. And I will put my
Spirit in you and move you to follow my decrees and be

careful to keep my law. Then you will live in the land I gave
your ancestors; you will be my people, and I will be your
God.
Ezekiel 36:26-28

God Prospers Us

God has it in His Heart for Us to Prosper. He has restored us to
Himself through Jesus Christ and has given us the power of Jesus'
resurrection living inside us. We can now know the mysteries that
were hidden because we are God's saints. We can live with the
assurance that Christ lives in us, the hope of glory. We can see God
is all about showing His glory:

> *...when He opened the fifth seal, I saw under the altar the*
> *souls of those who had been slain for the word of God and for*
> *the testimony which they held.*
> Revelation 6:9

No matter our purpose in life, we must do it to the fullness of Christ,
walking in Him, being:

> *...rooted and built up in Him and established in our faith*
> *as we have been taught, abounding in it with thanksgiving.*
> Colossians 2:7

If it is our purpose to be slain by sharing the gospel and our
testimony, are we still willing to do it for the Lord? Are we at the
place where we are not afraid of death but ready to live for Him and
die for Him at whatever the cost? Do we believe we are His and know
we can endure what we will go through because we belong to Him?

According to Colossians 2:10, it states, "You are complete in Him, who is the head of all principality and power." One day, "...every knee will bow, and every tongue will confess He is Lord."[207] The gospel is the power of God. It's the power that He gave us in His name, which is why *everything* will be cast out in His name. Jesus spoke these words:

> *"Behold, I give unto you power to tread on serpents and scorpions, and overall the power of the enemy: and nothing shall by any means hurt you."* - *Jesus*
> Luke 10:19

We have more power than we know and use. We have the authority within us to withstand anything that comes against us, even physically. Yet, we hinder the Holy Spirit by listening to others who do not understand the mind or the ways of Christ. Therefore, we are not to let anyone trick us:

> *...through philosophy and empty deceit, according to the tradition of men, according to the basic principles of the world, and not according to Christ.*
> Colossians 2:8

When the Israelites broke the law, it became a curse for them because they did not have the Holy Spirit in their hearts. They were to follow the law, but the rulers added more laws, which made it impossible to follow. When Jesus became that curse, He fulfilled the law, allowing us not to have to experience the cursed nature.

---

207   Philippians 2:10

Christ has redeemed us from the curse of the law, having become a curse for us (for it is written, 'Cursed is everyone who hangs on a tree') that the blessing of Abraham might come upon the Gentiles in Christ Jesus, that we might receive the promise of the Spirit through faith.
Galatians 3:13-14

For the life of the flesh is in the blood: and I have given it to you upon the altar to make an atonement for your souls: for it is the blood that maketh an atonement for the soul.
Leviticus 17:11

Our bodies make enough blood to live long lives, thanks to the Lord. It is by Jesus' blood that we are given an *atonement* for our souls. Our *atonement* means to be *reconciled* and *given amends for our wrongs.* God has given our atonement upon the altar of the cross. He fulfilled the requirements of the law because He is the lamb of God that was slain before the foundation of the world. His resurrection brought forth life. Therefore, He has the name above all names. It was for the whole world to see that He came for the world, for anyone who would accept Him and believe in Him.

God made him who had no sin to be sin for us so that in him, we might become the righteousness of God.
2 Corinthians 5:21

Those who believe in Him have been raised with Him, and now we are *over* the law, not being dead to it or subjected to it but able to overcome the sinful nature.

For we know that our old self was crucified with him so that the body ruled by sin might be done away with, that we should no longer be slaves to sin

because anyone who has died has been set free from sin.

Now if we died with Christ, we believe that we will also live with him.

For we know that since Christ was raised from the dead, he cannot die again; death no longer has mastery over him.

The death he died, he died to sin once for all; but the life he lives, he lives to God.

Romans 6:6-10

Therefore, we are slaves of God because we were bought with His blood, and our bodies are no longer their own.

In the same way, count yourselves dead to sin but alive to God in Christ Jesus.

Therefore do not let sin reign in your mortal body so that you obey its evil desires.

Do not offer any part of yourself to sin as an instrument of wickedness,

but rather offer yourselves to God as those who have been brought from death to life;

and offer every part of yourself to him as an instrument of righteousness.

For sin shall no longer be your master because you are not under the law, but under grace.

Don't you know that when you offer yourselves to someone as obedient slaves,

you are slaves of the one you obey-whether you are slaves to sin, which leads to death,

or to obedience, which leads to righteousness? You have been set free from sin and have become slaves to righteousness.

Now, offer yourselves as slaves to righteousness, leading to holiness.

But now that you have been set free from sin and have become slaves of God,

the benefit you reap leads to holiness, and the result is eternal life.
Romans 6:11-22

Now by this, we know that we know Him if we keep His commandments.

He who says, "I know Him," and does not keep His commandments, is a liar, and the truth is not in him.
But whoever keeps His word, truly the love of God is perfected in him. By this, we know that we are in Him.

He who says he abides in Him ought himself also to walk just as He walked.

Brethren, I write no new commandment to you, but an old commandment which you have had from the beginning.
1 John 2:3-7

The old commandment is the word which you heard from

the beginning. Again, a new commandment I write to you, which thing is true in Him and in you, because the darkness is passing away, and the true light is already shining.

He who says he is in the light and hates his brother is in darkness until now.

He who loves his brother abides in the light and there is no cause for stumbling in him.
1 John 2:7-10

We can tell if we are walking according to God's will for our lives because He promises we will not stumble. We must keep alert to know how we are standing in our faith and if we have picked up any offenses and are doing things in our own strength. Those that make excuses not to practice righteousness are not doing things God's way. It's a good way to discern if those you follow or listen to are born of Him.

> *"If you know that He is righteous,*
> *you know that everyone who practices*
> *righteousness is born of Him."*
> 1 John 2:29

To know who is born of Him can be confusing because many people preach we can do whatever we want because we live under grace. We must know what His grace has done for us, and when we act in love because of His grace. This way we can become more like Jesus because our faith will be growing. Faith to faith is an action. We cannot be all we are for God without spiritual growth.
He that believes and is baptized shall be saved. As soon as we are old

enough to understand and make decisions on our own, we should make the decision to get baptized. Even if we were baptized as an infant, it is still good to make the decision as an adult because as an infant our parents made the decision for us. Therefore, being baptized is a confession of our faith in Jesus Christ as our Lord and Savior.

> *"Let the message of Christ dwell among you richly."*
> Colossians 3:16

Our faith is more precious than gold. What will we have to offer Him besides that? Love motivates us to testify His love and mercy. We should be great representers of our faith and our Father.

> *...Be holy, for I am holy. And if you call on the Father, who without partiality judges according to each one's work, conduct yourselves throughout the time of your stay here in fear.*
> 1 Peter 1:16-17

Remember, a reverent fear of God is knowing He is with us, no matter where we are. When we do any *work*, we do it all unto Him even when we do good and suffer judgment, ridicule, criticism, and rejection. "When you do good and suffer, if you take it patiently, this is commendable before God."[208] *Patiently* means *remaining in conduct*, knowing God is still working on others, as well as you. Nobody is perfect. Always look from the other person's perspective before making harsh judgments and accusations. Embrace each other's differences. God made us all different for a reason. The more

---

208   1 Peter 2:20

we recognize and honor each other where we are in life by celebrating each other, the more unified we can become. Remember, even "...if you should suffer for righteousness' sake, you are blessed."[209] We must have it at the forefront of our minds that it's *not about us,* but it is about God and what He wants to do through us for His good pleasure.

> *Beloved, do not think it strange concerning the fiery trial which is to try you, as though some strange thing happened to you; but rejoice to the extent that you partake of Christ's sufferings, that when His **glory is revealed**, you may also be glad with exceeding joy.*
> 1 Peter 4:12-13

Our hearts need to be adjusted to what God is doing so we may receive the salvation of the soul, which is the eternal life we are promised when our faith stands the fiery test.[210] As the Lord, Himself said:

> *Do not lay up for yourselves treasures on earth. . . but lay up for yourselves treasures in heaven. . . For where your treasure is, there your heart will also be.*
> Matthew 6:19-21

Our soul is in question when we do not do what pertains to godliness, meaning, if we are not obedient to God and His Word. We are stealing the abundant life He has given us from ourselves. When we become determined, focused, and set our hearts on fire for Him, we see that time speeds up, but when we have no purpose, do things without

---

209   1 Peter 3:14
210   1 Peter 1:9

a vision, it seems as though our days are long. The reason why our time speeds up when we have purpose is because He promises to return the days of our youth, so our time is added to us, and we shall be rendered according to our righteousness.[211] We have the power to obtain greatness. The question is: are we willing to walk in the spirit, in love, and truth without wavering in our faith and stand to the very end?

"But he endures to the end
shall be saved."
Matthew 24:13

"Whom having not seen, you love;
in whom, though now you see him not,
yet believing, you rejoice with joy
unspeakable and full of glory:
Receiving the end of your faith,
even the salvation of your souls."
1 Peter 1:8-9

"Therefore, get rid of all moral filth and
the evil that is so prevalent
and humbly accept the word planted in you,
which can save you."
James 1:2

"Because you have made the LORD,
who is my refuge,
Even the Most High, your dwelling place.
No evil shall befall you,

---

211   Job 33:24, 2 Timothy 2:1

Nor shall any plague come near your dwelling;
For He shall give His angels
charge over you, to keep you in all your ways.
In their hands they shall bear you up,
Lest you dash your foot against a stone.
You shall tread upon the lion and the cobra,
the young lion and the serpent
you shall trample underfoot.
"Because he has set his love upon Me,
therefore I will deliver him;
I will set him on high,
because he has known My name.
He shall call upon Me,
and I will answer him;
I will be with him in trouble
I will deliver him and honor him.
And show him My salvation."

Psalms 91:9-16

REFERENCES

Alcott, Amos Bronson. *Good Health: A Journal of Hygiene*, Volumn 17. Battlecreek, Michigan. (1882 January 17).

Bragg, P. C., & Bragg, P. (2017). *The miracle of fasting: proven throughout history for physical, mental, and spiritual rejuvenation*. Santa Barbara, CA: Health Science.

Emoto, M. (2004). *The Hidden Messages in Water*. Hillsboro, OR: Beyond Words.

Fortune, M. M., & Fortune, M. M. (2002). *Violence in the family: a workshop curriculum for clergy and other helpers*. Cleveland, OH: Pilgrim Press.

Geisler, N. L. (1985). Colossians. In J. F. Walvoord & R. B. Zuck (Eds.), The Bible Knowledge Commentary: An Exposition of the Scriptures (Vol. 2, p. 680). Wheaton, IL: Victor Books.

Hadhazy, A. (2010, February 12). Think Twice: How the Gut's "Second Brain" Influences Mood and Well-Being.

Hille, S. (1985). The rod of guidance. FaithTrust Institute (Reprinted from *SCAN Advocate, Spring 1985*).

Johnson, Bill. (accessed 1/15/2020), <https://www.facebook.com/BillJohnsonMinistries/posts/if-you-dont-live-by-the-praises-of-men-you-wont-die-by-their-criticisms/10150181003393387/>

(n.d.). Retrieved from <https://www.ssib.org/web/>

Shelton, H. M. (1963). *The hygienic system vol. Ii: orthotrophy*. San Antonio, TX: Dr. Sheltons Health School.

Society for the Study of Ingestive Behavior. (2015, July 7). High fat diet changes gut microbe populations and brain's ability to recognize fullness. *ScienceDaily*. Retrieved December 27, 2019 from <www.sciencedaily.com/release/2015/07/150707212451.htm>

Wolchover, Natalie, Busting the 8-Hour Sleep Myth: Why You Should Wake Up in the Night, LiveScience <https://www.livescience.com/12891-natural-sleep.html>

Made in the USA
Las Vegas, NV
17 August 2021